TELONEON
PRESS

WHEN YOU ARE NOT IN THE ROOM

The Hidden Story of What You Are Really Building

Javier Castillo Gil

Teloneon Press

Published by Teloneon Press, an imprint of The Morphing Group

www.teloneonpress.com

ISBN (Paperback): 978-1-968540-00-5

ISBN (eBook): 978-1-968540-01-2

ISBN (Hardcover): 978-1-968540-02-9

Library of Congress Control Number: 2025916313

First Edition

Cover design by Samuel Andrés Castillo

Editor: Sarah Cisco

For more content and resources, visit:

www.morphing.guru/not-in-the-room

This book is a work of nonfiction. The insights and perspectives shared are based on the author's professional experience. The examples were drawn from real situations, with identifying details modified or omitted to preserve confidentiality. Any resemblance to specific individuals or organizations is unintentional unless explicitly acknowledged. The strategies and frameworks presented are for educational and informational purposes only and may not be appropriate for all circumstances. Readers are encouraged to seek the advice of qualified professionals when needed. The author and publisher disclaim any liability arising directly or indirectly from the use of this material.

This book is the first volume in *The Leadership Legacy Series*, a collection of works exploring the enduring principles, practices, and impact of leadership, teams and organizations

Advance Praise for
When You Are Not in the Room

"I've had the privilege of working with Javier, and without a doubt, this book clearly reflects his ability to convey a practical leadership approach that is deeply centered on people. What I value most is the way he combines intentionality with method: it's not just about good intentions, but about leading with clarity, structure, and purpose.

Javier reminds us that leadership is not an instinctive act or an innate trait, but a discipline that must be strengthened with data, tools, and concrete practices. His approach invites us to evolve as leaders not through momentary inspiration, but through consistency and the responsibility to create real and sustainable impact."

Héctor Orellana Brun
VP North Latam

"To lead is not to stand out, it is to sustain. It is to create the conditions for others to grow, even when you are no longer there. This book puts into words that powerful transition: the shift from proving yourself to building from real responsibility. Javier manages to ground the intangible nature of leadership in concrete practices that transform teams, cultures, and—above all—conscience."

Juliana Angarita Saldarriaga
CHRO | Executive Coach | Inner Leadership Embodiment Advocate

"I met Javier over 15 years ago through Rutgers' Executive HR Leadership Program, and he immediately stood out—not just for his sharp mind, but for his depth, humility, and genuine presence. He's one of those rare people whose absence is noticed as much as their presence is felt. His ability to connect, challenge, and inspire has made him an invaluable thought partner ever since.

When You Are Not in the Room captures Javier's philosophy perfectly. It's not about flashy leadership or performative charisma—it's about what truly lasts: the systems, values, and culture leaders build that continue to thrive long after they've stepped away. His approach is both deeply human and incredibly practical, and it's exactly the kind of thinking organizations need today—especially in times of complexity and change. This book is a gift for anyone who cares about leading with integrity and leaving behind something meaningful."

Kate Etinger
Chief People Officer

"What remains when you're no longer there?

When You Are Not in the Room redefines what it means to lead. Drawing on over two decades of hands-on consulting, Javier Castillo Gil offers a compelling framework focused not on presence or charisma, but on sustainability, clarity, and legacy.

Through practical tools and sharp insight, this book challenges outdated leadership myths and introduces a new standard: leaders aren't measured by their control while present, but by the resilience, culture, and capability that endure in their absence. Javier provides actionable practices to shift from ego-driven leadership to impact that scales—where direction is clear, capabilities are enabled, and value is activated.

For leaders who care about what lasts—not just what performs—*When You Are Not in the Room* invites a shift from visibility to sustainability. Written for senior executives and HR leaders shaping tomorrow's organizations, it offers a practical, experience-based path to redefine leadership as a discipline, not a trait.

This book equips leaders to build cultures and systems that thrive without them. With a clear roadmap around direction-setting, enablement, and long-term value, it moves leadership from a personal style to a lasting legacy.

It's not about being the most visible person in the room—it's about becoming the most valuable, even when you're not."

Hugo A. Lara García
Managing Partner & Board Advisor | Former CEO

To my parents, who taught me to lead and to serve.

Preface

This book brings together over 25 years of hands-on leadership experience, working alongside organizations, leaders, and teams through the complexities of change, growth, and execution. Throughout those years, I have been writing articles, conducting studies, and documenting the lessons learned from practice. These ideas have been the backbone of my work, tested and refined across countless hours helping clients around the world to navigate real challenges. Writing this book is about offering, in one place, the structure and clarity that have proven effective in practice. It distills years of leadership work into actionable insights: what has worked in boardrooms, on factory floors, and in team conversations where culture, clarity, and accountability were on the line.

I am fully aware that leadership, as a subject, has often been diluted into slogans, trends, and generalities. Much has been written and much has been oversimplified. This book is not an attempt to add to the noise. It is built from real experience inside organizations —as an employee, leader, consultant, and coach—witnessing firsthand the complex, human realities that leadership demands. What follows is not perfect or final; it is simply an honest attempt to illuminate the practical nuances that too often get lost, but which make all the difference in building sustainable leadership impact.

The frameworks and principles in this book were originally consolidated during my time building Working Knowledge Consulting Group. They were applied and refined through direct client work, and when I co-founded The Morphing Group (TMG), they became the starting point for a broader methodology. Today, these ideas continue to evolve as part of TMG's approach to leadership and organizational transformation—strengthened by the collective experience and application across industries and regions.

Though written in my voice, this book reflects the philosophy and foundation of our work at TMG. It is not a sales pitch. It is an invitation: to challenge assumptions, sharpen reflection, and deepen the practice of leadership in ways that endure beyond any one person's tenure.

Content

PART I: THE DECISION TO LEAD

PART II: LEADERSHIP IN MOTION

PART III: LEADING YOURSELF FORWARD

Introduction

Leadership remains one of the most discussed—and most misunderstood—topics in business today. As John Kotter (1990) argues in *What Leaders Really Do*, leadership is often confused with management, leading to misconceptions about its true role.[1] There is no shortage of books, frameworks, or theories on what it means to be a great leader. Yet companies still struggle with leadership, employees remain disengaged, and most leaders operate without a clear understanding of their actual role.

Part of the reason is that, for all the writing and research, essential nuances are still overlooked.

In many organizations today, leadership is treated more as a status—a title achieved rather than a responsibility assumed. This aligns with Warren Bennis' (1989) argument in *On Becoming a Leader*, where he states that true leadership is about character and competence, not just position.[2] Most people step into leadership roles because it is the next logical step in their career, not because they have consciously decided to take on the expectations that leadership requires. The corporate world reinforces this by rewarding people who drive short-term results, often at the expense of long-term success. Companies

---

[1] John P. Kotter, *What Leaders Really Do* (Boston: Harvard Business Review Press, 1990).
[2] Warren Bennis, *On Becoming a Leader* (New York: Basic Books, 1989).

promote leaders who push for performance *today* but fail to build the foundations necessary for sustained success *tomorrow*.

Leadership, however, is not just about holding a title. Some of the best leaders in organizations are not in formal leadership roles at all—they are the ones who help teams find clarity, enable capabilities to perform, and activate motivation and engagement. At the same time, many people in formal leadership positions hold the title, but they never actually lead in any meaningful way. The distinction between **formal** and **informal leadership** matters, and this book focuses on those in **formal leadership roles**: people who are **expected** to lead but often have little guidance on what that actually means.

> *Too many step into leadership as a promotion, not as a decision to lead.*

Leadership in a Changing World: Why the Fundamentals Still Matter

The world has changed. Remote work, AI, globalization, and evolving workforce expectations have transformed the way organizations operate. But while the tools and environments have shifted, the core practices of leadership **remain unchanged**.

Some argue that leadership today is different, that the hierarchical models of the past were effective for their time and that modern leadership must adapt to a new world. However, as Gary Hamel (2020) discusses in *Humanocracy*, rigid structures have long been a barrier to innovation, making leadership adaptability a necessity rather than a modern shift.[3] But leadership was never just about hierarchy; it has always been about clarity, enablement, and motivation.

In the industrial era, leadership could get away with being more command-driven because work was routine, employees were

---

[3] Gary Hamel and Michele Zanini, *Humanocracy: Creating Organizations as Amazing as the People Inside Them* (Boston: Harvard Business Review Press, 2020).

physically present, and interactions were more controlled. But even then, the best leaders—those who built sustainable success—understood that leadership was more than issuing orders.

What has changed is how visible poor leadership has become. In a hybrid or remote world, unclear direction is immediately crippling. A leader who fails to enable their team in an AI-driven workplace will quickly lose relevance. Leadership practices aren't needed more today than before; they have always been necessary. The difference is that, now, leaders who ignore them will be left behind— faster and more visibly than ever before.

This book is not focused on temporary leadership trends, it is about the fundamentals that have always mattered and will continue to matter. The way leaders apply them will evolve, but the core responsibilities of leadership remain the same.

The Leadership Confusion: Three Things That Get Mixed Up

One of the biggest reasons leadership is so misunderstood is that most discussions mix three fundamentally different concepts. Kouzes & Posner (2007), in *The Leadership Challenge*, emphasize that leadership is not about position or power, but about engaging in behaviors that create trust and enable performance.[4] Their work aligns with the idea that leadership is a set of practices rather than a function or style.

1. **Leadership Functions**—The core responsibilities that a leader must fulfill: direction-setting, decision-making, planning, organizing, selecting talent, managing execution, and control, to name a few. These are essential, but they do not define leadership by themselves.

---

[4] James M. Kouzes and Barry Z. Posner, *The Leadership Challenge*, 4th ed. (San Francisco: Jossey-Bass, 2007).

2. **Leadership Style**—The personality-driven aspects of leadership: whether someone is charismatic or reserved, autocratic or collaborative, analytical or intuitive. Many leadership books emphasize style, making people think they need to change their personality to be effective.

3. **Leadership Practices**—The actual behaviors that make leadership work: providing a clear and compelling direction, enabling capabilities, and activating talent to create value. Unlike functions (which are about job responsibilities) and style (which is about personality), practices are what leaders need to **do consistently** to be effective.

The problem is that most leadership discussions treat these as interchangeable. They are not. You won't get far trying to change someone's personality, but you can train them to be more effective at enabling their team. You cannot coach someone to be more charismatic in the same way you can coach them to provide clear direction. While it is possible to develop some leadership traits (like presence or confidence) it is significantly harder, requires deep personal commitment, and often does not yield the same impact as improving core leadership practices.

These three dimensions (Leadership Functions, Leadership Practices, and Leadership Style) are explored throughout the book. A visual model illustrating how they intersect to drive effectiveness is presented in **Figure I** (see Chapter 1).

While these dimensions are distinct, they are not optional. **Leadership effectiveness demands the integration of all three**: the leader must execute the required functions of the role, apply the right practices to engage others and build systems, and adapt their style to ensure the message lands. This is why the common phrase *"He's not a leader; he's just a manager"* is misleading—because leaders also manage. It's not about choosing one dimension over the others. Great leadership happens when the functions are performed well, the practices are embedded consistently, and the style is adapted thoughtfully.

Now, here's the thing: When we talk about leadership effectiveness, we have to ask—*what should the effect of a leader be?* That question shifts our attention from what leaders do to what they are meant to accomplish. And that, ultimately, is what companies should be measuring. The reason we invest in improving Functions, Style, and Practices isn't because development is the goal in itself. The goal is to ensure that, through these dimensions, leaders can actually deliver on what the role demands. Leadership effectiveness is about achieving the right outcomes. And as we'll explore in Chapter 1, those outcomes go far beyond immediate results.

This book focuses specifically on **Core Leadership Practices**—the repeatable, trainable, and impactful actions that separate effective leaders from ineffective ones—because they are the most often misunderstood or neglected. As Daniel Goleman (1995) emphasizes in *Emotional Intelligence*, great leadership is less about innate talent or technical skill alone, and more about mastering key behaviors that drive engagement, clarity, and execution.[5]

Leading in a Broken System: Why Organizations Set Leaders Up to Fail

Having worked specifically in leadership development for over two decades, I have seen firsthand how companies often fall short in defining what they truly expect from their leaders. Many organizations assume leadership is understood; yet, if you ask ten executives within the same company what leadership means, you will often get ten different answers. This inconsistency is not just a minor issue—it fundamentally shapes how leadership is practiced, developed, and rewarded. A company may claim to value collaboration, yet promote individuals based purely on personal performance. They may encourage innovation but punish mistakes harshly. Leaders do not

---

[5] Daniel Goleman, *Emotional Intelligence: Why It Can Matter More Than IQ* (New York: Bantam Books, 1995).

learn what is important from slogans or mission statements; they learn from the behaviors that are rewarded and the actions that are tolerated.

If leadership is so important, why do so many organizations have a hard time getting it right?

Because most companies don't actually know what they want from their leaders. They might say they want strong, visionary leaders who build great teams and enable long-term success. But they measure, reward, and promote based on short-term performance. The result? Leaders who optimize for immediate execution, often at the cost of their team's long-term effectiveness.

This creates a leadership paradox:

- Leaders are expected to think long-term, but they are rewarded for short-term wins.
- Leaders are told to build strong teams, but they are promoted based on individual performance.
- Companies want sustainable success, yet their incentive structures encourage short-term decision-making.

Most organizations do not take the time to formally define leadership. If you ask their executives what the company's definition of leadership is, you will likely get a variety of answers. There may be an informal understanding, but that is part of the problem—leadership is often defined not by deliberate agreement but by what the company rewards and recognizes. This disconnect leads to inconsistent leadership practices and unclear expectations.

This misalignment between what leadership should be and what companies reward creates a cycle where leaders chase immediate results, burn out their teams, and fail to build anything that lasts. Kouzes & Posner (2010), in *The Truth About Leadership*, argue that leadership is fundamentally about credibility, trust, and enabling others to act[6]—yet organizations often neglect to nurture these qualities in their leaders, focusing instead on short-term gains. Jeffrey Pfeffer (2015), in *Leadership BS*, critiques this exact issue, arguing that organizations often develop and reward leaders based on perception rather than effectiveness.[7]

Leadership That Outlasts You

There is a critical distinction between **short-term leadership** and **sustainable leadership**. Short-term leaders focus on immediate performance. Sustainable leaders focus on both performance today and what remains after they are gone.

Think about it this way: If you hold a leadership position for 5, 10, or even 15 years, that is still a fraction of the time that a company expects to be in business. Organizations aim for 100+ years of longevity. That means half of a leader's job is **delivering results today**, and the other half is **ensuring results long after they are gone**.

This is where most leadership development efforts stumble. The question is not just: *Are you achieving your goals today?* The real question is: *What will remain when you are no longer in the picture?*

- Have you built a team that can thrive without you?
- Have you institutionalized good decision-making and problem-solving?
- Have you developed leaders who can continue driving success?
- Have you strengthened the culture, or are you the glue holding everything together?

Most leaders never ask these questions, yet they define whether leadership is truly successful. This book will push you to rethink

---

[6] James M. Kouzes and Barry Z. Posner, *The Truth About Leadership: The No-Fads, Heart-of-the-Matter Facts You Need to Know* (San Francisco: Jossey-Bass, 2010).

[7] Jeffrey Pfeffer, *Leadership BS: Fixing Workplaces and Careers One Truth at a Time* (New York: Harper Business, 2015).

leadership beyond personal success—it will challenge you to lead in a way that **outlasts you**.

You might be thinking, "Whatever I leave behind will be the company's problem." That may be true. But if you are not concerned about the legacy you are building as a leader, then leadership might not be the right role for you.

Half of a leader's job is delivering results today, and the other half is ensuring results after they are gone.

The Challenge: Are You Ready to Lead Differently?

If you are looking for another book full of motivational quotes about leadership, this is not it. If you are looking for a book that will tell you leadership is about being inspiring and charismatic, this is not it.

This book is about **doing the actual work of leadership**. It will force you to confront the gaps in how leadership is practiced today, rethink what leadership actually means, and apply concrete practices that will make you more effective.

Leadership is not a title—it is a responsibility and a privilege. The only question is: Are you ready to take it on and do it right?

PART I: THE DECISION TO LEAD

Moving Beyond the Illusion

"THE PRICE OF GREATNESS IS RESPONSIBILITY."
— Winston Churchill

Chapter 1: Understanding the Leadership Role

Leadership is often misunderstood—not because people don't care about it, but because it is rarely defined clearly. Many step into leadership roles without questioning what it actually entails. For most, leadership is simply the next logical step in their career path. But leadership is not just a title, a promotion, or a recognition of past success. It is a responsibility and a privilege, one that requires intentionality, a shift in perspective, and an understanding of what being a leader actually means.

Throughout years of helping companies develop leaders, I've learned that the most critical starting point is to define the leadership role itself. The challenge, however, is that while leaders often have different interpretations of what their role involves, companies themselves rarely take the time to align on a clear definition. Leadership is a term so commonly used that many assume there is a shared understanding when, in reality, perspectives vary widely, shaped by long-held beliefs about what makes a 'great leader.'

Rather than beginning with the question of what a leader is, I suggest starting with a more fundamental one: What should a leader accomplish? This shift in perspective moves leadership from a vague concept to a tangible role with measurable outcomes. Only by clarifying what leaders are responsible for achieving can we define what leadership should truly be.

The Organizational Failure to Define Leadership

What Great Leadership Actually Achieves

If organizations struggle to define what leadership is, they struggle even more to define what leadership is supposed to accomplish. This is not a semantic issue—it's a strategic one. When leadership is only judged by short-term results, we reduce its purpose to execution. But the real question should be: *What should happen when leadership is effective?*

Understanding what leaders must do is essential. But those actions—Functions, Practices, and how they are delivered through Style—are a means to an end. Leadership effectiveness should be evaluated based on what those actions enable. In my time working with executives and leadership teams across industries and cultures, I've consistently observed that truly effective leadership delivers four critical outcomes:

> *You can't build leadership with intention if the blueprint is missing.*

1. **Extraordinary Results:** At its core, leadership must ensure that strategy turns into execution. This includes meeting business objectives, delivering performance consistently, and maintaining operational discipline. Leaders who cannot achieve results lack credibility. But leaders who focus only on results often miss what makes those results sustainable. Execution is necessary, but it's not sufficient.

4

2. **Organizational Fluidity:** Results can be achieved in dysfunctional ways, through fire drills, heroics, or pressure. Effective leadership removes that friction. It builds systems that operate efficiently—with clarity, coordination, and momentum. I call this *fluidity*: the ability for things to move forward without bottlenecks, waste, or unnecessary escalation. Leaders are responsible not just for the outcomes, but for the way those outcomes are achieved. Fluidity means people can do their best work without constant interference or workaround.

3. **Value Creation:** Some leaders keep the system running. Others make it better. Leadership that creates value goes beyond maintaining the status quo—it challenges it. It means improving processes, enabling innovation, spotting risks before they escalate, and acting on opportunities others don't see. Value creation happens when a leader empowers people to think differently and makes room for ideas to evolve into impact. In stagnant systems, leadership protects what exists. In effective ones, it helps what's next to emerge.

4. **A Thriving Culture:** No outcome is more tied to long-term sustainability than culture. Effective leadership builds an environment where people can grow, contribute, and commit. This includes putting the right people in the right roles, ensuring alignment to purpose, developing talent intentionally, and reinforcing shared behaviors. A thriving culture is not about perks or slogans—it's about the energy people bring to their work, their sense of belonging, and the belief that their contributions matter. Leaders who ignore this foster compliance. Leaders who prioritize it enable commitment.

These four outcomes (results, fluidity, value creation, and thriving culture) form the real scoreboard for leadership effectiveness. They are what leadership is meant to accomplish when Functions are executed well, Practices are embedded consistently, and Style is used intentionally. As we will see next, the three dimensions leaders must align are the levers that make these outcomes possible.

The Distinction Between Functions, Practices, and Style

Leadership effectiveness depends on aligning what a leader does with what leadership is meant to achieve. These actions can be organized into two core disciplines: **Leadership Functions** and **Leadership Practices**. Both represent what a leader must *do*, but they serve different purposes and timelines. Functions focus on executing the role effectively; Practices focus on building the conditions for long-term success. A third dimension, **Leadership Style**, reflects not what a leader does, but *how* they do it. Rooted in personality traits and behavioral preferences, Style influences the effectiveness of both Functions and Practices.

These three dimensions—Functions, Practices, and Style—form the foundation of what defines *Leadership Effectiveness*. Each plays a distinct but interconnected role. Leadership Functions represent the operational responsibilities required to deliver outcomes. Leadership Practices are the consistent behaviors that create the conditions for long-term success. Leadership Style reflects the leader's individual traits and preferences that shape how they execute those Functions and Practices. Together, these dimensions determine not only what a leader does, but how sustainably and effectively they lead.

I have used this concept frequently in response to a recurring challenge I observe when working with leadership frameworks across organizations and cultures: Most of them present leadership as a unified concept, yet they conflate operational functions, behavioral practices, and personality traits. This lack of distinction creates confusion. Leaders are left asking: *Is leadership about what I do, how I behave, or who I am?*

In practice, all three elements matter, but they must be clearly defined. Through years of observation, research, and practical application, I identified consistent leadership gaps that could not be explained by style or role expectations alone. What became clear is that **certain core practices—regardless of culture, industry, or context—are frequently neglected** and that sustainable leadership effectiveness depends on intentionally developing them.

While this book gives particular emphasis to Leadership Practices, it's important to clarify that no single dimension is sufficient on its own. Effective leadership requires the synchronization of all three: executing the Functions of the role competently, applying Practices consistently to create the right system and environment, and using one's Style intentionally to adapt and connect. Leaders often default to one dimension based on their background or comfort zone—analytical leaders might overemphasize function, while relational leaders may lean heavily on style. But Leadership Effectiveness is not achieved through strength in one area; it's achieved through the integration of all three. You cannot create long-term value if you only manage operations well but fail to engage others; nor can you inspire with style if your execution falters. This book focuses on Practices because they are most often underdeveloped, but it is their alignment with the other two that makes a leader truly effective.

Introducing the Leadership Effectiveness Model: A Blueprint for Sustainable Leadership

To lead effectively, it's not enough to be action-oriented, well-intentioned, or even highly experienced. Leaders must understand the mechanics of their role, what they do, how they do it, and why it matters. Without that clarity, development becomes reactive, fragmented, and shallow. Leadership cannot remain a vague ideal; it must be broken down into distinct, teachable disciplines that can be refined with intention.

The Leadership Effectiveness Model does exactly that. It maps the three essential dimensions of leadership (**Functions**, **Practices**, and **Style**) and shows how their alignment drives sustained performance. By connecting what leaders execute with how they behave, and how those behaviors influence people and systems, the model provides a coherent blueprint for building leadership that delivers results, creates value, fosters a thriving culture, and works fluidly through others.

Let us briefly address what each dimension is about and the role they play in your effectiveness.

Leadership Functions refer to the operational aspects of the role—strategy setting, decision-making, planning, organizing, managing execution, and configuring the team by selecting the right talent. These functions are essential for achieving immediate business results, ensuring goals are met, and maintaining efficient operations. While they primarily serve short-term objectives, many also contribute to mid-term success by sustaining stability and execution over time.

Unlike leadership practices, which are behavioral and system-building in nature, functions are closely tied to role expectations and vary by professional background. A CFO is expected to master financial oversight, just as a CMO must lead with market insight. These actions are not just intuitive—they are learnable and trainable, often developed through formal education, structured workshops, or accumulated experience. Over time, the depth and quality of execution in these functions reflect both a leader's career path and the maturity of their operating context.

Leadership Practices, on the other hand, are the strategic behaviors that enable long-term sustainability. They ensure that beyond short- and mid-term performance, the organization continues to evolve, talent grows, and leadership capacity is built for the future. Unlike leadership functions, these practices are not tied to a specific role or professional background—every leader, regardless of function or level, must develop them. They focus on building a culture and system where execution remains strong even in the leader's absence.

While leadership practices can be taught conceptually, their mastery depends far more on real-world application, reflection, and feedback. Because they involve human dynamics—like influence, communication, development, and trust—they are nuanced and situational. This is why many leaders struggle: they may understand the theory, but they lack the deliberate practice needed to adapt these behaviors to different people, contexts, and organizational conditions. Still, these practices are the cornerstone of sustainable leadership effectiveness. Without them, even the best-executed strategies will fall short of long-term impact.

Leadership Style: The Role of Personality in Leadership Effectiveness. Personality traits undeniably influence leadership effectiveness. Every leader brings their own style and behavioral tendencies into their role, it's unavoidable. However, what differentiates effective leaders is not their personality itself, but their ability to understand how their natural preferences and behavioral biases impact their leadership practices. Rather than attempting to change their personality, leaders should focus on how to adapt their approach to ensure their practices are effective.

Consider giving feedback as an example—a fundamental leadership practice. While every leader must practice it, the way they deliver feedback will naturally vary based on their personality. Some may be direct and assertive, while others may take a more reflective or diplomatic approach. Neither one is inherently better nor worse; what matters is whether the feedback achieves the desired impact. The effectiveness of feedback also depends on the personality and receptiveness of the recipient. A leader who lacks self-awareness may unintentionally deliver feedback in a way that doesn't resonate—even if their intentions are good.

This is why self-awareness is critical. Leaders who understand their natural tendencies can consciously adapt their approach to ensure their leadership practices(such as feedback, coaching, or providing a clear direction) are executed in a way that maximizes impact. The practice itself remains the same—feedback must be given, but the delivery should be adapted to fit both the leader's style and the needs of their team.

The model that follows brings these insights together by distinguishing and integrating the three dimensions required for effective leadership.

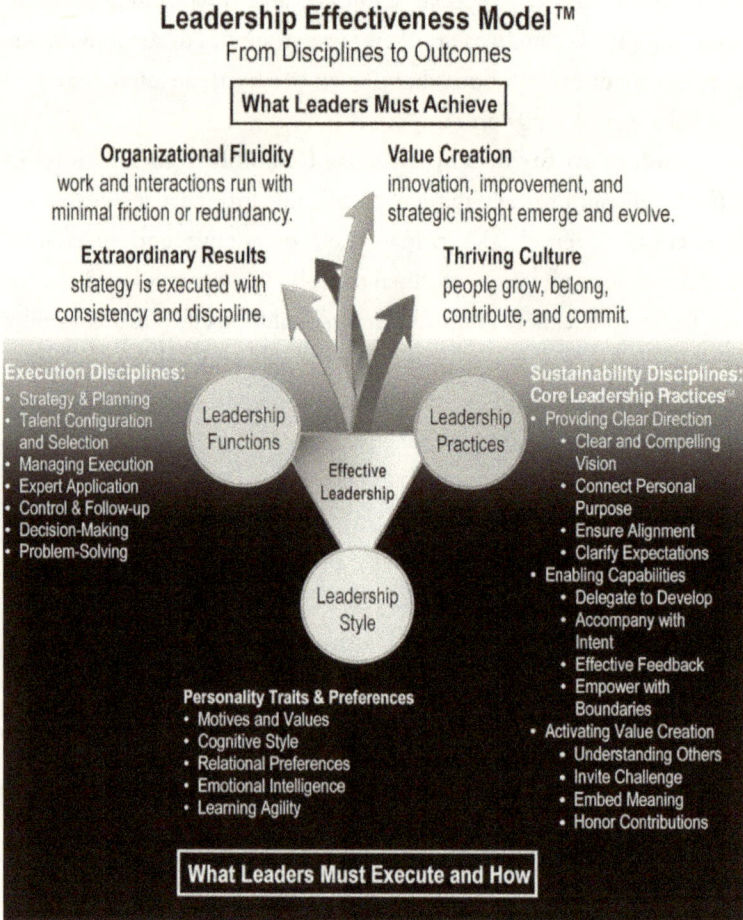

Leadership Effectiveness Model™
From Disciplines to Outcomes

What Leaders Must Achieve

Organizational Fluidity
work and interactions run with
minimal friction or redundancy.

Value Creation
innovation, improvement, and
strategic insight emerge and evolve.

Extraordinary Results
strategy is executed with
consistency and discipline.

Thriving Culture
people grow, belong,
contribute, and commit.

Execution Disciplines:
- Strategy & Planning
- Talent Configuration and Selection
- Managing Execution
- Expert Application
- Control & Follow-up
- Decision-Making
- Problem-Solving

Leadership Functions

Leadership Practices

Effective Leadership

Leadership Style

Sustainability Disciplines:
Core Leadership Practices℠
- Providing Clear Direction
  - Clear and Compelling Vision
  - Connect Personal Purpose
  - Ensure Alignment
  - Clarify Expectations
- Enabling Capabilities
  - Delegate to Develop
  - Accompany with Intent
  - Effective Feedback
  - Empower with Boundaries
- Activating Value Creation
  - Understanding Others
  - Invite Challenge
  - Embed Meaning
  - Honor Contributions

Personality Traits & Preferences
- Motives and Values
- Cognitive Style
- Relational Preferences
- Emotional Intelligence
- Learning Agility

What Leaders Must Execute and How

Figure I. **The Leadership Effectiveness Model: From Disciplines to Outcomes**
Leadership effectiveness results from aligning what leaders do—through Functions and Practices—with how they do it—through Style. When executed intentionally, these disciplines drive four essential outcomes: results, fluidity, value creation, and a thriving culture.

Understanding the Importance of Each Dimension

Beyond daily functions, leadership's effectiveness should be measured by the environment it creates—one where people, performance, and progress continue to thrive, even in the leader's absence. Influence in leadership does not stem from authority alone, but from credibility, trust, and the ability to enable others. Leaders who focus only on task direction may secure compliance, but those who invest in people and vision generate lasting engagement—the foundation for sustained success.

The real measure of leadership isn't personal achievement. It lies in the capability and growth of the team. The strongest indicator of great leadership is not how well the leader executes, but how capable others become under their guidance. Can the team operate without constant direction? Are they proactive, accountable, and developing into leaders themselves? Strong leaders build systems that ensure long-term success—results, efficiency, value creation, and cultural resilience—even after they're gone. In contrast, leaders who micromanage or chase short-term wins create dependency, eroding both individual potential and organizational capacity.

A study by The Morphing Group (2023) found that organizations with strong leadership practices experience at least 25% higher employee engagement than those with weak or inconsistent leadership.[8] This confirms that effectiveness must be judged not just by short-term output, but by enduring impact on people, systems, and culture.

> *To assess a leader's impact, don't look at them – look at the team they've built.*

One example of this gap is when I ask sales directors about their role.

---

[8] The Morphing Group, *Key Findings on Sustainable Success: 2023 Study on Engagement, Leadership and Flow. Part 1 of 2* (January 2024), https://morphing.guru/resources.

Most mention hitting targets. Some add strategy or coordination. Rarely does someone describe their role as attracting the right talent, guiding them effectively, and growing their contribution. But that's the work—because when done well, it leads to all four leadership outcomes: extraordinary results, organizational fluidity, value creation, and a thriving culture.

Basic Misconceptions and Transition Challenges

Leadership Is Not About Authority–It's About Responsibility and Enabling Strong Capabilities

One of the most common misconceptions is that leadership is about authority—the right to make decisions, give orders, enforce discipline, and ensure goals are met. While authority may come with the role, leadership is about much more than that. True leadership is about influence, not control. More importantly, leadership is about enabling others to succeed. The correct measure of a leader is not in their personal achievements but in the effectiveness and growth of the people they lead, which is the clearest path to organizational sustainability. If leadership were only about achieving personal success, organizations could operate with a group of highly skilled individual contributors and no leadership structure at all. But great leaders are necessary because they guide, develop, align, and empower others to reach new levels of performance. The sustainability of results depends on their ability to make others shine.

People follow great leaders not because they have to, but because they believe in what they can achieve under their guidance. Leadership goes beyond being admired for your greatness—it's about helping others envision and reach their own. People engage with leaders who create opportunities for growth, learning, and success—leaders who make them feel valued and included in something greater than themselves. True followership is not obedience; it is a

12

commitment to a shared vision and a belief that the leader will help them reach their full potential.

And before you think we are going down the rabbit hole of a romantic view of leadership, let's be clear: Engagement, growth, and fostering an environment where people thrive aren't just "nice-to-haves"—they are essential for sustainable business success. Leaders who neglect these aspects might achieve short-term gains but will struggle to build a resilient and high-performing organization over time.

Why Many Step Into Leadership Without Understanding It (And Why Most Companies Get It Wrong)

Most professionals move into leadership because they excel in their technical or functional roles. As Ram Charan explains in *The Leadership Pipeline*, many organizations fail to distinguish between managing work and leading people, often promoting individuals based on past performance rather than leadership potential.[9]

This transition can be jarring. The skills that made them successful in their previous role—deep technical knowledge, individual problem-solving ability, and personal execution—are no longer the primary skills they need to succeed as leaders. Leadership requires a different mindset: one that prioritizes enabling others over personal execution.

Yet, most organizations neglect preparing new leaders for this shift. This challenge is well-documented by leadership experts, including renowned leadership thinker, Marshall Goldsmith in *What Got You Here Won't Get You There*, who highlights how the very behaviors that drive individual success often become obstacles in

---

[9] Ram Charan, Stephen Drotter, and James Noel, *The Leadership Pipeline: How to Build the Leadership Powered Company* (San Francisco: Jossey-Bass, 2001).

leadership roles.[10] Without intentional development, leaders battle to adapt, finding themselves trapped in old habits that no longer serve their new responsibilities.

I have seen countless professionals promoted into leadership roles, only to grapple with the realization that their job is no longer about their personal expertise, but about empowering others. This gap leaves many leaders frustrated, feeling as if they are pulled away from "real work" because they now have to conduct feedback sessions, coaching conversations, and development planning—things they often perceive as HR-driven tasks rather than core leadership responsibilities.

Knowing When to Let Go

Some years ago, I had the opportunity to coach a newly appointed CEO. He had been an outstanding VP of Sales—driven, strategic, and known for getting things done. When he took on the CEO role, he was excited about the opportunity, ready to lead with energy and determination.

But within months, signs of strain began to show across the organization. His involvement in commercial decisions remained as strong as ever—he would challenge the new Head of Sales on her decisions, criticize marketing's positioning, and openly voice his frustrations about production bottlenecks. Three clear problems emerged.

First, he was still thinking like the Head of Sales, not the CEO of the company. His deep engagement in commercial matters made his executive team feel that sales always had the upper hand. Other departments—finance, marketing, and production—felt sidelined, their decisions constantly overruled or deprioritized.

---

[10] Marshall Goldsmith, *What Got You Here Won't Get You There: How Successful People Become Even More Successful* (New York: Hyperion, 2007).

Second, the new Head of Sales felt undermined. She fought to assert authority over her own team because the former VP of Sales—now her CEO—was still stepping into sales matters, sometimes reversing her decisions. To make matters worse, her team quickly realized that they could bypass her entirely and go straight to the CEO for approvals, since they knew he would ultimately be the one making the final call anyway. Instead of strengthening her leadership, his continued interference eroded her authority and made it harder for her to lead effectively.

Third, and most critically, his leadership was unintentionally creating structural problems. Sales had become emboldened to bypass internal processes, knowing they had the CEO's backing. Support functions (finance, compliance, and HR) were showing signs of burnout as they tried to enforce controls that sales was routinely circumventing. The company was becoming less fluid, less collaborative, and less balanced.

When I began working with him, the company's HR Head said to me: *"He's a great guy, he gets things done... and somehow, the company is suffering."*

That became the focal point of our conversations: **What does 'getting things done' really mean?**

In his mind, success meant hitting revenue and financial targets. But the real measure of leadership at the CEO level isn't just financial performance—it's creating an environment where the company thrives sustainably. It's ensuring that collaboration works across departments, that talent develops, that teams are empowered rather than micromanaged, and that innovation isn't stifled by short-term pressures.

The hardest lesson for him wasn't about strategy or execution—it was **learning to let go.** The strengths that had propelled him to this level (his ability to challenge the status quo, fight for resources, and push past internal obstacles) had become derailers in his new role. The company no longer needed him to be the best VP of Sales; it needed him to be the CEO.

And that's where organizations also fall short. Rarely do they take the time to clearly define what they actually expect from their leaders beyond financial metrics. Leadership at every level requires a shift in mindset. The higher you rise, the further into long-term sustainability you must think. But that shift doesn't happen unless the leader—and the company—are aligned on what leadership success looks like.

You Can't Develop What You Haven't Defined

According to Future Market Insights (2025), the global leadership development program market is projected to grow significantly over the coming decade, with an estimated value of $89.5 billion in 2025, expected to surpass $235 billion by 2035.[11] The United States remains one of the most prominent markets, with recent analyses placing its 2024 value at approximately $6.8 billion, and projections suggesting it could exceed $12.4 billion by 2034.[12] Despite this growth, organizations continue to struggle with building a strong and sustainable leadership pipeline, often investing heavily in development without addressing the underlying dynamics that shape effective leadership.

This disconnect is echoed in recent data, showing that organizations continue to face significant challenges in cultivating effective leaders. Gallup's *State of the Global Workplace 2024* report reveals that leadership, particularly at the managerial level, plays a critical role in shaping employee engagement.[13] The report highlights that managers experienced the sharpest decline in engagement, dropping from

---

[11] Future Market Insights, *Leadership Development Program Market Size & Trends 2025–2035,* June 5, 2025, https://www.futuremarketinsights.com/reports/leadership-development-program-market.
[12] Expert Market Research, *United States Leadership Development Program Market Size & Share 2034,* accessed June 10, 2025, https://www.expertmarketresearch.com/reports/united-states-leadership-development-program-market.
[13] Gallup, *State of the Global Workplace 2024* (Washington, DC: Gallup, 2024), https://www.gallup.com/workplace/393497/world-trillion-workplace-problem.aspx.

30% to 27%, which in turn has a cascading effect on their teams' engagement levels. This underscores just how central leadership effectiveness is to overall employee engagement. Furthermore, Gallup notes that only 44% of managers globally have received formal management training. This lack of preparation contributes directly to the challenges managers face in effectively leading their teams.

Similarly, the 2023 DDI Global Leadership Forecast found that 77% of organizations report a leadership gap, with only 11% confident in their leadership bench strength.[14] These findings point to a troubling reality: While leadership is widely recognized as vital to organizational success, many companies still fall short in preparing leaders who can effectively engage and inspire their teams.

This isn't because leadership development isn't a priority—it's because the way companies approach and invest in leadership development is fundamentally flawed.

I have observed that many organizations struggle to develop strong leaders not because of a lack of investment, but because they haven't clearly defined what leadership actually is. Without a shared understanding of the core responsibilities, behaviors, and outcomes that define leadership effectiveness, development efforts become fragmented—focused on surface-level skills, abstract traits, or isolated events with little impact.

One of the most persistent challenges in leadership development is the lack of distinction between the dimensions of leadership itself. When Leadership Functions, Practices, and Style are treated as a single, undifferentiated concept, development efforts reflect that confusion. Models and programs often blend these dimensions without clarifying what belongs where—presenting leaders with a mix of responsibilities, behaviors, and traits as if they were all developed in the same way. But they are not. Each dimension demands a different learning approach: Some require technical training, others behavioral

---

[14] Development Dimensions International, *Global Leadership Forecast 2023* (DDI, 2023), https://www.ddiworld.com/global-leadership-forecast-2023.

practice, and others deep self-awareness and reflection. When these are collapsed into one framework—or worse, one session—leaders walk away without clarity, unable to identify where to focus or how to grow. The result is not just conceptual overload, but ineffective development.

You cannot build leadership with intention if the blueprint is missing. Leadership, like any discipline, must first be clearly articulated through a coherent framework, before it can be cultivated with purpose and consistency.

Leadership training is often centered on classroom-based programs, seminars, and theoretical coursework, assuming that leadership can be taught in isolation from real-world experience. However, leadership is not developed through lectures alone. It must be learned on the job, through structured coaching, real-world application, and alignment with the company's broader systems and expectations. Without these practical, experience-based learning mechanisms, leadership training becomes just another corporate exercise—informative, but ineffective in creating lasting behavioral change.

Because of this, I have often seen leaders define "what leadership means" based on their own past experiences rather than through a structured developmental process. In my work with executives, I frequently hear them describe their leadership approach as a reflection of what they observed under previous bosses—sometimes emulating strong role models but often replicating flawed or outdated practices. When companies don't take the time to clearly define what leadership should look like, leaders default to what they know—even when it's ineffective.

If organizations truly want effective leadership, they must go beyond promoting high performers and instead develop leadership capabilities with intention. This means:

- Clearly defining what leadership means within the company.
- Equipping new leaders with the necessary skills to succeed beyond just their technical expertise.

- Integrating leadership development into daily work, rather than isolating it in workshops and seminars.
- Align company practices on rewards, promotions, and recognition with leaders' ability to deliver the key outcomes of leadership—results, fluidity, value creation, and a thriving culture.

Companies should move beyond traditional classroom-based leadership programs and invest in structured coaching, mentorship, and leadership development integrated into real work experiences. Leadership isn't learned in a one-time seminar—it must be practiced, guided, and reinforced in real-world situations. Without this, even the best theoretical training will be unable to create real, sustainable leadership effectiveness.

Only by doing so can organizations create leaders who don't just deliver results today but also build the foundation for sustainable success.

Leadership isn't learned in a seminar – that's like trying to fly a plane after just reading the manual.

Looking Ahead: Breaking Leadership Myths

If leadership is about enabling others and delivering long-term value—through results, fluidity, innovation, and a thriving culture—why do so many leaders still fall short? The answer lies in long-standing myths that continue to distort how leadership is understood and practiced. These misconceptions shape behaviors, influence promotion decisions, and embed themselves in organizational systems—often rewarding control, charisma, or short-term wins over real effectiveness.

In the next chapter, we will challenge these myths directly and examine how they continue to undermine leadership performance. Only by deconstructing these assumptions can we begin to reframe what great leadership truly looks like—and why it must be built differently.

Chapter 2: The Leadership Hamster Wheel

Monkey See, Monkey Do

My son has always been passionate about his beliefs. He has grown into a resourceful thinker and an avid critic of the status quo. From a young age, he has challenged ideas, asked bold questions, and offered strong opinions that often sparked memorable conversations—especially around what is right and wrong. When he was nine, he came home from school visibly upset.

I asked him what was wrong, and he angrily responded, *"They picked David as class president!"*

Curious, I asked him why he was so upset about it.

He responded, "Because he's the popular kid, and the worst part now is that everyone agrees we have to do whatever he says—after all, he's the class president!"

There it was—his group's understanding of leadership at that moment: being in charge meant controlling others. No one had explained to the class what the actual role of the president was supposed to be, so they had assumed. The election was based on popularity, not on leadership ability, and they all believed that the person chosen would now be above the rest of the class, not in service to it.

This isn't just a childhood misunderstanding—it's a corporate reality.

Across industries, companies select, reward, and promote leaders based on deeply ingrained myths about what leadership should look like. These myths are so embedded in corporate culture that they dictate who rises to the top—even when those individuals lack the practices needed to truly lead.

The result? A self-reinforcing system—The Leadership Hamster Wheel—where the same types of leaders keep getting promoted, even when their leadership proves ineffective. In this chapter, we will explore five common leadership myths, why companies reinforce these misconceptions, and how organizations can break the cycle by redefining leadership with intention.

> *When leadership is left undefined, people will fill in the blanks – and often get it wrong.*

The Five Myths That Distort Leadership

Misconceptions about leadership don't just come from individuals; they are embedded in organizational cultures. Companies don't define leadership properly, so people create their own definitions, often based on flawed assumptions. Here are five myths that continue to distort how leadership is perceived.

Myth 1: "Great Leaders Are Born, Not Made"

One of the oldest and most damaging leadership myths is the idea that leadership is an innate quality—something a person is either born with or will never have. Under this belief, leaders emerge naturally, and those who do not have "it" will never be capable of leading effectively.

The reality is that leadership is not a genetic trait; it is a set of learned behaviors. While certain personality traits—such as confidence, decisiveness, or charisma—may make leadership more natural for some individuals, effective leadership is developed through deliberate practice, self-awareness, and experience.

Some of the greatest leaders in history weren't natural-born leaders—they became great through learning, adapting, and refining their approach. Organizations that fail to develop leadership as a practice fall into the trap of only promoting those who seem like "natural" leaders, overlooking those who could become highly effective if properly trained.

When the leadership role is not fully understood, leaders often fall into the trap of entitlement—believing they deserve their position rather than focusing on the responsibilities that come with it. Thoughts like *"Someone thought I was good enough to be here, so I must act like it"* or *"The company expects me to shine, that's why they put me in this position"* start shaping their behavior. While confidence in one's abilities is important, leadership isn't a quest for personal validation—it's a commitment to delivering on expectations.

And that's where the real challenge lies: If those expectations aren't clearly defined, leaders may unknowingly neglect the very practices that create long-term impact and organizational stability.

I often refer to this as the "Finalized Product Syndrome"—a mindset I frequently observe in appointed leaders. They assume that being given the role is clear evidence that they have already proven themselves. But in reality, taking on a leadership position should never be seen as an affirmation of having "arrived." Every leadership role comes with new challenges, different dynamics, and unpredictable variables. Each team is unique, and the same leadership approach that worked in one situation may not be effective in another. The best leaders recognize that leadership is learned, not granted, and that every step up is an opportunity to be reinvented—to refine one's approach, to adapt to new realities, and to deepen one's understanding of how to lead effectively.

Leadership is not a fixed state—it is an ongoing process of learning and growth. The moment a leader assumes they have nothing left to learn, they risk becoming stagnant, unable to evolve with their teams and the organization. Great leadership is not about being the best—it's about continuously becoming better.

Myth 2: "Leadership Is About Making Big Decisions"

Many people equate leadership with decision-making power. The assumption is that the leader must always have the answers, must be the final authority on all matters, and that leadership success is measured by their ability to make the "right" decisions.

While decision-making is important, leadership is not just about making choices—it is about creating an environment where good decisions happen consistently. A leader who tries to make every decision alone quickly becomes a bottleneck, limiting team autonomy and slowing progress.

Great leaders do not just make decisions—they create systems where teams are empowered to make sound decisions on their own. Leadership means guiding and enabling capabilities in your people, rather than positioning oneself as the sole source of answers.

This myth also leads people to mistakenly believe that admitting *"I don't know"* or *"I don't have the answer for that"* weakens their authority. But avoiding such vulnerability ultimately harms their leadership more than it protects it. Leaders who feel compelled to always have the right answer risk closing themselves off to other perspectives, limiting their ability to listen, invite suggestions, accept feedback, and learn from mistakes.

This mindset also creates an unintended consequence: It fosters dependency. When a leader positions themselves as the ultimate decision-maker, their team members become conditioned to delegate upwards, waiting for the *all-knowing leader* to provide the perfect solution. Over time, this not only slows down decision-making but also weakens the organization's problem-solving capability. Worse still, some leaders thrive on this dynamic, enjoying the feeling of being indispensable. However, this dependency creates a high-risk scenario for the company—one in which leadership effectiveness is concentrated in a single individual, making the organization vulnerable if that leader is absent, leaves, or simply fails to adapt to new challenges.

Leaders are not eternal, as we have discussed before. Their true role is not to be the source of every decision but rather to create an environment where sound decisions can be made—even in their absence. That is the real test of sustainable leadership.

Myth 3: "The Best Leaders Are Highly Charismatic"

It is easy to assume that leadership requires magnetic presence—that great leaders must be naturally persuasive, inspiring, and larger than life. This is a dangerous assumption.

Charisma might make people listen, but it does not guarantee effective leadership.

There are some great leaders in business history who are not naturally charismatic or extroverted, yet they have shaped industries through strategic thinking, consistency, and an ability to inspire through action rather than showmanship. The assumption that great leaders must be highly expressive and magnetic overlooks the fact that many of the most effective leaders succeed through methodical decision-making, quiet confidence, an unwavering commitment to long-term vision, and being extraordinary at leadership practices.

Take Tim Cook, for example. Unlike his predecessor, Steve Jobs—who was known for his electrifying stage presence and larger-than-life personality—Cook's leadership at Apple has been deliberate, process-driven, and operationally disciplined. He is not a showman, nor does he seek the spotlight. Instead, he focuses on creating a culture of strong execution, operational excellence, and long-term strategic focus. Under his leadership, Apple has become more financially robust, increased its supply chain efficiency, and expanded its product ecosystem beyond what many thought possible—all without relying on charisma to rally his team.

What makes Cook's leadership effective is that he has strengths in all three fundamental leadership practices:

1. **Providing Clear Direction** → Cook is known for his strategic clarity. While Jobs was the visionary, Cook translated that vision into an operational reality by ensuring that Apple's long-term direction remained intact while refining its execution. His focus on sustainability, privacy, and supply chain efficiency provided Apple with a steady, long-term direction that employees could align with.

2. **Enabling Capabilities** → Cook avoids micromanagement. Instead, he has built one of the most capable leadership teams in the world, giving them autonomy while holding them accountable for excellence. He actively fosters a culture where leaders within Apple have the space to innovate and take ownership, rather than needing his constant intervention.

3. **Activating Value Creation** → Under Cook's leadership, Apple has broadened its product and service offerings, moving beyond hardware to a services-driven ecosystem (Apple Music, Apple TV+, and iCloud). He has activated new areas of value by leveraging Apple's core strengths, demonstrating that a leader's job is not just maintaining what exists, but creating new opportunities for impact.

Similarly, Warren Buffett has built one of the most successful investment empires in history, not by being a forceful or grandiose leader, but through methodical analysis, unwavering discipline, and a commitment to clear and simple decision-making. Buffett is not known for flashy speeches or commanding boardroom presence. Instead, his calm, rational, and deeply analytical approach to leadership has made Berkshire Hathaway a gold standard for sustainable business growth. His influence comes not from charisma, but from trust, wisdom, and a proven ability to guide others through sound principles and long-term thinking.

Buffett's leadership also embodies the three core practices:

1. **Providing Clear Direction** → Buffett is known for communicating in simple, clear terms. His annual shareholder letters are famous for their straightforward explanations of complex financial strategies, ensuring that employees, investors, and stakeholders understand the company's direction without corporate jargon.

2. **Enabling Capabilities** → Buffett famously empowers the CEOs of Berkshire Hathaway's subsidiaries, giving them autonomy to run their businesses without excessive oversight. He places high trust in his leadership teams and believes in hiring great people, setting expectations, and then getting out of their way—a hallmark of true leadership enablement.

3. **Activating Value Creation** → Buffett's investment philosophy is centered on long-term value creation rather than short-term speculation. He doesn't just invest in companies—he guides them to enhance their strengths and maximize their potential. By prioritizing long-term value over short-term gains, he ensures that his leadership impact endures well beyond any single market cycle.

These examples challenge the myth that leadership is all about personality and presence. While charisma can be an asset, it is not the defining trait of effective leadership. Great leaders earn influence not by dominating the room, but by fostering clarity, making sound decisions, and ensuring that their teams and organizations thrive in a structured, sustainable way.

Organizations that equate leadership with charisma tend to promote the wrong people, favoring those who command attention rather than those who enable success. Effective leadership should be measured by sustainable impact, not popularity.

Myth 4: "Leadership Is About Authority and Control"

Many still believe a leader's job is to be in charge—to ensure that rules are followed, tasks are assigned, and that they enforce discipline. This mindset leads to micromanagement, control-driven environments, and low team engagement.

Effective leadership isn't about controlling people—it's about creating the conditions for success. Leaders who cling to authority create cultures where employees hesitate, disengage, and avoid accountability. The best leaders set clear direction, provide support, and trust their teams to execute. Rather than enforcing control, great leadership fosters an environment where people take ownership.

Many companies resist this approach, fearing that without strict oversight, mistakes will multiply and performance will decline. However, trusting teams to execute does not mean handing over the keys to the kingdom and retreating to a throne. Effective leadership involves striking a balance between autonomy and accountability—providing the clarity, support, and structure necessary for people to take ownership of their work.

Consider the ongoing debate around remote work. Many leaders assume that if employees work remotely, they will procrastinate, juggle multiple jobs, or spend their time improving their golf handicap. While those risks exist, they are not a function of remote work itself but rather a symptom of poor leadership. When expectations are vague, accountability mechanisms are weak, and leaders fail to track meaningful progress, performance issues arise—regardless of where people are physically located.

In my experience, the real problem isn't that remote employees take advantage of flexibility—it's that many organizations lack the courage to address underperformance when it happens. Accountability doesn't require constant supervision; it requires clear expectations, measurable goals, and structured follow-through. A well-led team—whether in-person or remote—knows exactly what is expected of them, understands how their work is measured, and has a leader who ensures that outcomes are delivered. A leader's role is not to hover over every task, but to set the conditions where performance is both expected and enabled. Anything less is simply a lazy approach to leadership.

As we mentioned earlier, the evolving business landscape does not require a different kind of leadership—it reinforces the need for leadership practices that have always been essential: enabling and developing others. However, in a world increasingly shaped by AI and rapid innovation, leaders who rely on control and authority will strain more than ever. The capabilities that an AI-driven organization unlocks demand agility, collaboration, and adaptability—qualities that controlling leaders inadvertently suppress.

In today's hyper-competitive environment, the illusion of control is more damaging than ever. Leaders must recognize that attempting to micromanage every aspect of innovation and growth is a losing battle. Instead, their role is to clear the path for value creation—ensuring that people have the autonomy, resources, and alignment necessary to contribute meaningfully. A better measure of leadership is not how much a leader controls, but how effectively they create conditions for others to thrive within the strategic vision they set.

Myth 5: "Leaders Should be Chosen Based on Performance"

Perhaps the most common misconception in leadership selection is the belief that the best individual contributors make the best leaders. Companies assume that high performers will naturally transition into leadership roles.

But leading a team requires an entirely different skill set than executing tasks. Without preparation, these individuals struggle with delegation, coaching, and strategic thinking—often defaulting to doing everything themselves rather than leading.

Even individuals who have already begun their leadership journey in lower management roles have much to learn as they step into more complex corporate positions. A frequent mistake is assuming that past performance is a reliable predictor of future success—but that assumption only holds true if the conditions remain the same. The reality is that moving into a new leadership role means navigating a different environment, with new challenges, broader responsibilities, and a diverse set of stakeholders. What worked in a previous role may not necessarily translate into success in the next.

This misunderstanding is particularly evident in how organizations approach High-Potential (HiPo) employees. Too often, they are treated as "plug & play" leaders—expected to seamlessly transition into higher roles based on their past success. Ironically, it is precisely that past success that can become a derailer. Leaders who have been promoted because of strong performance receive an implicit message: *"Since you are great, we want you to take on this new role."* Naturally, their instinct is to replicate the behaviors that made them successful before. However, leadership progression is not about repeating past formulas—it requires self-awareness, adaptability, and situational thinking.

Every leadership role demands a unique balance of skills, and stepping into a new position often requires developing new competencies, relinquishing outdated behaviors, and embracing a different approach. Without proper guidance, even the most talented leaders risk defaulting to old habits that may no longer serve them

Leadership fails when past results are mistaken for future readiness.

well. This is why leadership transitions must be accompanied by structured coaching, clear expectations, and an understanding that growth in leadership comes not from doing more of the same, but from evolving with each new challenge.

When companies promote based solely on past performance, they set their leaders up for failure. Without the necessary preparation, support, and recalibration of expectations, these leaders often falter, unknowingly undermining their teams and stalling long-term success. A strong leadership pipeline isn't built by rewarding past achievements—it is forged by intentionally developing leaders who can adapt, grow, and elevate those around them. Failing to recognize this leads not just to individual setbacks, but to organizational stagnation.

The Leadership Hamster Wheel: Why Companies Keep Picking the Wrong Leaders

Because companies neglect to define leadership properly, they unknowingly create a pattern in how they select and promote leaders. This creates The Leadership Hamster Wheel—a system where certain leadership types are promoted, even when they are not equipped to lead effectively.

Four Key Leadership Stereotypes That Get People Promoted

You've likely encountered people in your career who seem to embody the qualities of a leader. But that perception is often shaped by unconscious bias—if your company hasn't clearly defined what leadership truly entails, your idea of a leader is likely based on personal experiences and assumptions rather than an objective standard.

When we hold a preconceived notion of what a leader should look like, it becomes easy to be misled by surface-level traits—behaviors that may signal leadership but don't necessarily equate to effective leadership. If someone talks like a leader, walks like a leader, and reacts like a leader, then they must be a leader, right? Well, that depends entirely on what you believe leadership is.

This is precisely why leadership should be measured by outcomes, not appearances. Even the most charismatic or commanding presence means little if a leader is unable to create a team that knows what's expected of them, aligns with a shared vision, and continues to grow and perform—even in their absence. Effective leadership isn't about dependency; it's about building sustainability. The most impactful leaders don't just guide their teams in the present—they ensure that success continues long after they are gone.

Companies suffer from this the same way that we all do—after all, decisions about who to promote are really taken by other people in leadership positions, so they also have their own unconscious bias. There are four key leadership stereotypes that usually get people into the promotion chair. I want to be clear, the company needs all these types of individuals to create change, deliver results and evolve, but none of them by themselves make effective leaders:

1. The Achiever—The Relentless Performer

This is the leader who gets things done. They are highly assertive, take control of situations, and push for results. They thrive in crisis management, tolerate uncertainty, and are often seen as the problem-solvers of the organization.

Why They Get Promoted:
- They deliver fast, tangible results and often act as firefighters in difficult situations.
- They take control when things are unclear or chaotic.
- They project confidence and a "can-do attitude," which organizations love.

How They Usually Derail Without Leadership Practices:
- They struggle to delegate, believing no one can do it better than them.
- They burn out their teams, expecting everyone to operate at their level of intensity.
- Their leadership style doesn't scale—they create dependency instead of empowerment.

2. The Change Agent—The Visionary Disruptor

The Change Agent is the big thinker, always challenging the status quo and pushing for innovation. They are risk-takers, bold in their decisions, and have an instinct for what's next.

Why They Get Promoted:
- They bring fresh perspectives and position themselves as innovators.
- They challenge outdated processes and drive major transformations.
- They exude passion and confidence, making them compelling leaders on the surface.

How They Usually Derail Without Leadership Practices:
- They focus too much on change and not enough on execution.
- They move too fast for the organization, frustrating teams who feel left behind.
- They fail to bring people along with them, making their ideas hard to implement.

3. The Networker—The Charismatic Connector

This leader is magnetic, socially skilled, and well-connected. They build strong relationships and know how to rally people behind an idea. They are natural influencers, often energizing and inspiring teams.

Why They Get Promoted:
- They create excitement and momentum within the organization.
- They attract talent and maintain a wide internal and external network.
- They present well and easily project confidence that simulates leadership strength.

How They Usually Derail Without Leadership Practices:
- They enjoy the spotlight but find it difficult to share, making it hard for others to shine.
- They focus on perception over substance, sometimes lacking depth in execution.
- They are great motivators but poor coaches—they generate excitement but fail to develop talent.

4. The Expert–The Technical Mastermind

The Expert is the intellectual powerhouse—a deep specialist in their field. They are analytical, detail-oriented, and highly knowledgeable, often sought after for their expertise.

Why They Get Promoted:
- They have unmatched technical expertise and are seen as the go-to authority.
- They solve complex problems with precision and logic.
- They maintain high standards and enforce strong discipline and rigor.

How They Usually Derail Without Leadership Practices:
- They prioritize knowledge over people, assuming that being right is more important than coaching others and allowing them to make mistakes and learn.
- They have a hard time trusting non-experts, often micromanaging or resisting delegation.
- They struggle to develop talent, preferring to execute tasks themselves instead of enabling their team.

Why These Stereotypes Are Not Enough

Each of these leadership types adds value. I have met many of them and you can't help but be enchanted by their respective skills and overwhelming domain in their own terrain. The critical point to understand is that, while useful, none of these traits automatically make someone an effective leader. There is real danger when companies confuse these traits with leadership itself.

Without adopting the right leadership practices, these strengths can become weaknesses.

- The Achiever must learn to enable others, not just deliver results themselves.
- The Change Agent must bring people along, not just drive transformation.
- The Networker must focus on substance, not just perception.
- The Expert must invest in developing others, not just being right.

When leadership is defined by short-term impact, these stereotypes continue to dominate. That's why companies keep promoting the wrong people—reinforcing a cycle of leadership failure—and remain trapped in their hamster wheel.

Each of these leadership stereotypes stands to benefit from adopting effective leadership practices, though they will naturally find some easier to adopt than others. Their ability to lead effectively is closely tied to their personality traits, which influences how they approach leadership. Through multiple interactions and assessments of leaders, I have observed that each of these stereotypes correlate with specific personality tendencies.

This is what makes leadership practices so powerful—they can be executed by anyone, regardless of their personality or dominant style. The challenge is that different leaders will find different leadership practices more difficult depending on their natural inclinations. If we are serious about leadership development, the key is not just to acknowledge these tendencies but to work through them.

The real success factor lies in self-awareness—helping leaders understand their strengths, recognizing how those strengths might become derailers, and developing an intentional approach to leadership. This requires guiding them to see what effective leadership practices look like, particularly focusing on those that are most difficult for them. It's not about changing personality—as some leadership books suggest—since that is often a fool's errand. Nor is it about blindly focusing on strengths, since these are precisely what can lead to derailment when overused. Instead, it's about making a conscious commitment to the actual work of leadership, turning effective leadership practices into habits, and executing them consistently—regardless of personal preferences.

> *Leadership practices aren't about changing who you are – they're about choosing how you lead.*

How Companies Can Break the Cycle

To escape The Leadership Hamster Wheel, companies must take deliberate action. As with any major change, the first step is acknowledging whether your organization is trapped in this cycle. If your company is one of the rare exceptions that already promotes leadership in a way that truly balances short- and long-term success, then congratulations—your leadership culture is ahead of the curve.

For the vast majority of organizations, however, this is a wake-up call. Recognizing the problem is essential, but change only happens when there is genuine commitment to implementation. Too often, leadership transformation becomes a philosophical exercise—a great discussion on leadership principles that never translate into meaningful action. If companies truly want to break this cycle, they must be willing to put their money where their mouth is.

The steps required to shift leadership culture are simple, but not easy. They require commitment, oversight, and relentless follow-through. More importantly, they demand a long-term focus—an acknowledgment that the goal is not just immediate results, but the sustainability of the company through enablement and leadership legacy.

Leadership practices are often dismissed as "soft skills," but in reality, if they are soft, they are the hardest to develop. Without a structured approach to reinforcing leadership behaviors, even the most well-intentioned leadership initiatives will fade over time. Companies that are serious about creating sustainable leadership must take decisive action, and that starts with rethinking how they define, develop, and reward leadership.

There are some key steps you should consider to start moving your company in the right direction:

1. **Redefine Leadership Expectations:** *Move beyond charisma, performance, or seniority and define leadership based on impact and effectiveness.*

   Many companies still select leaders based on the outdated assumptions we discussed, such as:

   o   Charisma → Mistaking likability and confidence for leadership ability.

   o   Seniority → Assuming that time in a role automatically translates to leadership readiness.

   o   Performance → Promoting top individual performers without assessing their ability to lead others.

   Studies from McKinsey and Harvard Business Review indicate that leaders who prioritize enabling others drive higher long-term organizational success than those solely focused on personal achievement.[15][16] Leadership effectiveness should be

---

[15] Michael Bucy, Bill Schaninger, and Brooke Weddle, "The Science Behind Successful Organizational Transformations," *McKinsey & Company*, April 2015, https://www.mckinsey.com/capabilities/people-and-organizational-performance/our-insights/successful-transformations.

[16] Jack Zenger and Joseph Folkman, "How Managers Drive Results and Employee Engagement at the Same Time," *Harvard Business Review*, June 2017, https://hbr.org/2017/06/how-managers-drive-results-and-employee-engagement-at-the-same-time.

measured by the impact on their team's development, alignment, and engagement—not just their own results.

A Test of Conviction

While consulting for a financial services conglomerate on defining their leadership expectations, I witnessed a pivotal test of their commitment to those standards. One of their top executives clearly violated the principles of effective leadership we had outlined—his behavior was inappropriate and counterproductive to a healthy work environment. However, he was also one of the company's highest performers in terms of financial results.

By traditional measures, he was delivering—hitting targets, driving revenue, and meeting short-term financial goals. But beneath the surface, the costs were undeniable. His leadership style and lack of effective leadership practices created a toxic work environment, resulting in high talent turnover and a culture of fear that stifled innovation. People hesitated to challenge decisions, and the long-term sustainability of the team was eroding.

Despite recognizing the issue, the company hesitated. Letting go of someone who produced strong financial outcomes—at least on paper—wasn't an easy decision. Eventually, they made the right call and removed him from the role, though it took longer than it should have. In the short term, there was a dip in financial performance, but the hidden costs they had been absorbing (talent loss, disengagement, and missed opportunities) had already far exceeded that temporary setback.

Defining leadership expectations isn't just about words on a page; it demands accountability. Upholding leadership standards requires courage: the willingness to make tough decisions that prioritize long-term organizational health over short-term gains.

2. **Develop Leadership as a Practice:** *Create a learning environment for leadership practices to improve skills like coaching, enabling capabilities, activating talent, and building sustainable execution systems.*

Leadership is not an innate trait—it is a set of behaviors that must be practiced and refined. Yet, many leadership development programs focus on knowledge, not execution. Sitting through a seminar on coaching doesn't mean a leader knows how to have difficult conversations, provide constructive feedback, or empower their team.

A well-known study by The Center for Creative Leadership found that 70% of leadership development happens on the job, while only 10% is from formal training.[17] Leadership must be developed through structured, on-the-job coaching—not just in classrooms.

Develop or Decay

There is a fundamental misunderstanding about the cost of leadership training. Many companies view it as an operational expense—something to be minimized or avoided—rather than a capital investment in the company's long-term sustainability. But just as you invest in new machinery or infrastructure improvements, investing in leadership is an investment in the core engine of your company: its people. Leaders shape engagement, culture, work environments, and ultimately, business results. Their influence extends far beyond their individual performance, impacting everyone around them.

One of my clients once resisted investing in leadership development, arguing that it was a "waste of money" because employees might leave, taking the company's investment with them. I challenged him to consider the cost of poor leadership, the disengagement, high turnover, and loss of innovation that stemmed from not developing his leaders. If we already acknowledge that most leaders

[17] Center for Creative Leadership, "The 70-20-10 Rule for Leadership Development," *Leading Effectively*, accessed April 25, 2025, https://www.ccl.org/articles/leading-effectively-articles/70-20-10-rule/.

will only remain in their roles for a decade at most, one might argue that investing in them is futile. But that mindset is rooted in the same flawed short-term thinking that undermines long-term success. The real question isn't "What if we invest in them and they leave?" but rather "What if we don't—and they stay?" Would you rather have mediocre leaders at a lower cost, or high-performing leaders who create a thriving environment that outlasts their tenure, even if they eventually move on?

A clear example of this came from a client in the spirits industry who decided to invest heavily in a small group of high-potential leaders. Instead of relying solely on traditional training programs, we helped them implement a personalized, in-house support program with sessions over 12 months. These sessions included real-time observation of the leaders in their work environment, assessing their interactions with teams, and guiding them as they implemented leadership practices. Unsurprisingly, the leaders showed clear improvement with such dedicated support. But what was even more remarkable was the ripple effect. These leaders didn't just improve individually, they began coaching and mentoring their peers, spreading the practices they had learned. As people saw tangible improvements and role models emerged, a tipping-point effect took hold, gradually transforming the company's culture.

In the long run, the impact of that investment far exceeded the initial cost. Developing leadership as a practice isn't just about improving individuals: it's about creating a systemic change that elevates the entire organization. Real leadership development shouldn't be seen as a luxury; it's a strategic necessity for any company that prioritizes long-term success.

3. **Change Promotion, Rewards, and Recognition Criteria:** *Reward and Recognize leadership behaviors, and measure leadership impact, not just individual performance. Make sure your company is being congruent with the established expectations and act accordingly.*

Most companies unintentionally reinforce the wrong leadership behaviors by promoting and rewarding the wrong things. If leadership promotions are based purely on performance, then high performers will continue to rise—even if they are terrible leaders.

Gallup's landmark 2015 *State of the American Manager* study found that 82% of companies fail to select the right people for leadership roles, a problem still echoed in recent research.[18] This persistent failure is largely due to promotion systems that prioritize individual results over leadership capability. When companies reward short-term performance without evaluating leadership behaviors or long-term impact, they unintentionally undermine the very culture they're trying to build.

The Value of Being Seen

I've witnessed firsthand how organizations that adjust their promotion criteria to include leadership behaviors experience a dramatic shift in their leadership culture—but only when they ensure that company policies, practices, and processes are aligned to support this change. Many companies instinctively turn to compensation and bonuses as the primary way to incentivize leadership behaviors. While understandable, I caution anyone against relying too heavily on financial incentives, especially before developing a mature understanding of the leadership role.

Compensation should always be tied to clear performance indicators, and while variable pay can certainly include leadership effectiveness beyond financial results, money alone is a myopic way to

---

[18] Gallup, *State of the American Manager: Analytics and Advice for Leaders* (Washington, D.C.: Gallup, Inc., 2015), 12, https://www.gallup.com/services/182138/state-american-manager-report.aspx.

drive leadership excellence. Meaningful recognition extends far beyond receiving a paycheck. Great leaders are motivated by opportunities, work-life balance, inclusion, learning, and professional growth—factors that contribute to engagement and reinforce leadership behaviors in a more sustainable way.

For example, while consulting for a pharmaceutical company, we conducted an in-depth analysis of their leadership population and discovered that middle managers valued acknowledgment and inclusion more than monetary rewards. Instead of defaulting to a traditional "employee of the month" approach, we designed a recognition system that provided aspirational opportunities. Leaders who received outstanding ratings from their teams were invited to speak at annual conferences or deliver TED-style talks within the company, sharing their experiences and insights with other units. This not only reinforced best practices but also created a learning culture where leaders inspired their peers. More importantly, the opportunity to be recognized publicly for their impact created an aspirational effect—others wanted to be next in line, not for the paycheck, but for the acknowledgment and influence it provided.

This is just one example of how companies can go beyond financial incentives to reinforce leadership behaviors in meaningful ways. Recognition, visibility, and opportunities for growth often carry more weight than bonuses, fostering a leadership culture that is driven by impact rather than short-term rewards. The key is to get creative—designing recognition systems that align with what truly motivates your leaders while reinforcing the leadership behaviors that will sustain the company's success.

If we keep rewarding what leadership is not, we'll keep building what we don't want.

Looking Ahead: Moving from Myths to Leadership Practices

Debunking these leadership myths is only the first step. The real challenge lies in replacing outdated assumptions with effective leadership behaviors that drive long-term success. It's not enough to recognize what leadership is *not*, leaders must understand what leadership *is* and, more importantly, how to practice it daily.

In the next chapter, we move from misconceptions to execution, introducing the three fundamental leadership practices that define truly effective leadership. These practices aren't tied to personality, character, or seniority—they are measurable, teachable, and, when applied consistently, create the conditions for sustainable success. Leadership earns its value not through status or individual brilliance, but through the ability to provide clear direction, enable capabilities, and activate value, the three **Core Practices of Leadership™** we explained at the beginning of this book.

If we want to break the cycle of poor leadership, we must move beyond theoretical ideals and focus on what leaders must actually do to create sustainable results, by building thriving teams and organizations. In Chapter 3, we will outline the foundation of leadership as a practice, setting the stage for how leaders at every level can develop and apply these principles effectively.

Chapter 3: Leadership as a Set of Practices, Not an Identity

The Coolest Job in the World?

My daughter has always been inquisitive, curious about the world and full of imagination, often challenging conventional thinking with idealistic perspectives. When she was seven years old, she came to me with a school assignment that required her to answer a simple question: *What does your daddy do?*

At the time, I was deeply involved in growing my consulting firm, transforming organizations by working on leadership and organizational effectiveness. So, after a brief pause, I told her:

"I help leaders become the best version of themselves."

She tilted her head and asked, *"What do you mean? What does a leader do?"*

I thought for a moment and then responded with the simplest, most honest answer I could give:

"They should make sure other people become extraordinary."

Her eyes lit up, and without hesitation, she said:

"That must be the coolest job in the world!"

That moment stuck with me. She saw something that many seasoned professionals often overlook: Leadership isn't about personal power or status—it's about elevating others.

But the reality in most organizations is very different. Leadership is often perceived as an achievement, a status, or a recognition of past success. Many leaders see their roles as a reflection of their personal worth rather than a responsibility to elevate others. Instead of focusing on how to make their teams better, they focus on proving their own competence, protecting their authority, or achieving short-term success at any cost.

This fundamental misunderstanding is why so many incumbents in leadership positions don't actually lead. It's why leadership feels so broken in many organizations. I am not suggesting that leadership is always rewarding or easy. It comes with hurdles, pressures, and responsibilities that can feel overwhelming. But when done right, leadership is a force for transformation—not just for the leader, but for everyone around them.

The Purpose of Leadership

One of the biggest reasons leadership is misunderstood is that its true *purpose* is rarely discussed. Many organizations neglect to provide clarity on leadership expectations, but beyond clarity, there's an even deeper issue: many leaders never stop to consider *why* they lead.

Yes, leadership is about driving business results, short and long term—but if that's the only focus, then we reduce leadership to a transactional function. The real power of leadership lies in its ability to create impact beyond oneself. It is a role where you can influence lives, shape outcomes, and build something that outlasts you. It is the space where you can achieve, transcend, and leave a mark—not just in financial statements, but in people's growth, success, and aspirations.

Now, **I know I've said before that this is not a romanticized view of leadership, and I stand by that**. You don't need to have a higher calling to be a better version of yourself as a leader. You don't need to believe in a grand purpose to execute leadership effectively.

If you follow the right practices (if you provide clarity, enable capabilities, and create value) you will still be a better leader than most.

But here's the thing: *Why you lead* is different from *how you lead*. You can be as structured and pragmatic as you like in your execution. You can be analytical, methodical, even cold in your approach—so long as you focus on the right practices, your leadership will be more effective.

That said, leaders who connect their role to a higher purpose—beyond just performing effectively—often create a greater impact. A clear purpose not only strengthens commitment but also attracts and retains top talent, making it easier to inspire and mobilize people toward a shared vision. While leadership effectiveness starts with practicing the right behaviors, purpose acts as a powerful amplifier, turning good leadership into truly transformative leadership.

Leadership is one of the few roles in which you *can* make a real difference in people's lives. You don't have to seek that impact, but if you choose to, it's there. The privilege of leadership gives you the ability to elevate others—not just because it's the *right* thing to do, but because, in the long run, it makes your organization more resilient and sustainable while allowing you to create a personal, more rewarding legacy.

So, if you ask me whether leadership is a cool job, my answer is simple: *It definitively can be, but only if you do it right.*

Moving Beyond Titles and Personalities

We've established that leadership is not an identity—it is not about charisma, knowledge, drive, or making big decisions. It is a responsibility that must be executed with intention.

Yet, leadership books and corporate programs continue to focus on who leaders should be, rather than what leaders should accomplish and how they should lead. There is endless discussion about leadership traits, personality types, and whether certain characteristics make someone a natural leader. But these debates miss the point entirely.

Leadership isn't about being a certain type of person, it's about practicing the right behaviors that drive results through others. You don't have to be naturally charismatic, visionary, or even extroverted to be an effective leader. You just have to do the work of leadership.

That is both liberating and challenging.

- It's **liberating** because it means anyone—regardless of personality—can become a better leader if they commit to the right practices.

  This idea is often met with skepticism, particularly from those who view leadership as an exclusive skillset only a select few possess. But given that most people in organizations I have assessed rate more than half of their leadership population as mediocre or worse, the need for a shift in perspective is clear.

  The oversimplified distinction between a "boss" and a "leader" reinforces the idea that leaders are either transactional managers focused only on outcomes or inspirational figures who engage and elevate their teams. Leadership is not a binary trait—it exists in a broad spectrum of effectiveness.

  A manager who is currently uninspiring or disengaged can significantly improve if provided with the right guidance, if they understand that leadership is not a theoretical construct but a set of concrete, actionable practices that can be learned and developed.

- It's **challenging** because it removes the excuses. If leadership is about behaviors rather than personality, then every leader is responsible for developing those behaviors—no matter their natural inclinations.

  I often present this challenge to leaders during workshops: *The kind of leader you are is entirely up to you.* There is no justification for being an ineffective leader—not your company's shortcomings, not your boss's limitations, not your personality. Leadership is a choice. And like any discipline, achieving mastery requires deliberate effort, self-awareness, and a commitment to continuous improvement.

*If leadership is about what you do—not who you are—
then being ineffective is a decision, not a destiny.*

Leadership Is a Discipline, Not an Instinct

People often assume that great leadership happens naturally—that good leaders simply "get it." But leadership is not an instinct. Yes, some people may naturally exhibit leadership tendencies, but leadership is less about innate talent and more about deliberate practice. What sets great leaders apart is not just their instincts but their commitment to consistently providing clear direction, enabling capabilities, and activating value within their teams. The best leaders aren't just those with natural ability—they are those who intentionally refine their approach over time.

This idea is not exclusive to leadership. In his book *Talent is Overrated (2008)*, Geoff Colvin examines how world-class performers in fields ranging from music to athletics to business succeed not only because of innate ability, but because they engage in deliberate practice—a structured approach to improving performance through continuous learning and effortful repetition.[19] Leadership follows the same principle: The most effective leaders are not simply born with exceptional leadership instincts; they commit to developing, refining, and applying leadership behaviors deliberately over time.

Consider how we develop any complex skill:

- A doctor isn't great simply because they have the "right personality" for medicine. They follow rigorous training, study best practices, and hone their craft through hands-on experience.

---

[19] Geoff Colvin, *Talent Is Overrated: What Really Separates World-Class Performers from Everybody Else* (New York: Portfolio, 2008), 66.

- A pilot doesn't rely on instinct alone. They follow precise procedures and even have to complete hundreds of hours of simulator training before attempting to command an aircraft.
- Even world-class athletes, regardless of their natural talent, follow structured training programs, receive coaching, and dedicate themselves to continuous improvement.

Leadership is no different. It requires effort, repetition, self-awareness, and course correction. And just like any discipline, the more you practice it correctly, the better you can become.

That said, leadership development has a unique challenge that some professions do not: It must be learned in real life.

A doctor can practice surgery on cadavers before ever operating on a live patient—and even then, she will have experienced mentors guiding her during the first complex procedures. A pilot spends countless hours in a simulator before ever taking flight and must fly with an instructor before commanding a plane solo. An athlete trains behind closed doors, perfecting their movements and having practice rounds before facing real competition.

So why do we treat leadership differently? Why do we assume that a newly appointed leader should step into their role and immediately succeed without structured coaching or real-world practice?

As many people who have experienced this before would attest, most key aspects of leadership can't be fully understood until they are experienced. You don't know what it feels like to fire someone until you do it. You don't understand the intensity of delivering tough feedback until you are face-to-face with an employee who isn't meeting expectations. And no amount of classroom training can truly prepare you for the weight of making high-stakes decisions in a critical board meeting.

Yes, role-playing and simulations can help new leaders prepare, but any leader who has been through these moments will tell you this: They are far more difficult than expected when faced in real life.

And this is precisely why leadership must be developed intentionally, not left to chance. Leaders need structured guidance, real-time coaching, and an environment that allows them to learn without risking total meltdown at the cost of their teams and organizations. Research supports this approach: effective leadership is not developed through passive learning but through real-world application. The *Oxford Research Encyclopedia of Business and Management* highlights that experiential learning is fundamental to leadership development, emphasizing that leaders cultivate their skills most effectively through active engagement, problem-solving, and reflection on real challenges, rather than through theoretical instruction alone.[20]

When leadership is treated as a skill—something that is practiced, refined, and improved—organizations begin to shift from hoping leaders will "figure it out" to ensuring they succeed.

Reframing Leadership: Understanding the Practices that Matter

Most leaders begin their day thinking about what needs to get done: the meetings they will attend, the decisions they need to make, the problems they need to solve, the targets they need to hit. They define success based on execution: Did we close the deal? Did we resolve the issue? Did we hit our numbers?

But leadership is not just about what gets done *today*—it is about ensuring the organization continues to thrive *tomorrow*.

---

[20] D. Christopher Kayes and Anna B. Kayes, "Experiential Learning and Education in Management," *Oxford Research Encyclopedia of Business and Management*, Oxford University Press, published online August 31, 2021, https://oxfordre.com/business/display/10.1093/acre-fore/9780190224851.001.0001/acrefore-9780190224851-e-294.

What a Company Needs from Its Leaders

If you ask a company, "Who is responsible for achieving financial results?" the answer is simple: executives, department heads, front-line managers—everyone has a role in delivering results.

But now ask:

- Who is responsible for creating an engaging culture that retains top talent?
- Who ensures that departments communicate and collaborate effectively?
- Who is accountable for fostering innovation, pushing the company forward, and keeping it one step ahead of the competition?
- Who develops the next generation of leaders to sustain the business beyond today?

The reality is organizations need leaders to step up in all these areas. Yet, most leaders are never explicitly held accountable for them.

The default assumption in many companies is that these things will happen naturally—that culture will "evolve," that collaboration will "improve," that the right talent will "emerge." But without intentional leadership, none of these critical elements are guaranteed.

The Leadership Equation: Equalizing Today's Execution with Future Success

This is where most organizations need to focus: defining leadership expectations beyond immediate execution. At its core, the Leadership Equation clarifies what leadership must integrate to create lasting impact. It illustrates that results are not driven by execution alone, but by the combination of role-based performance (Functions), consistent leadership behavior (Practices), and the enabling environment (Organizational Support). When these elements work together, leaders don't just deliver outcomes—they build the conditions for performance that endures. As shown in Figure II, effective leadership demands not just individual contribution, but also organizational support — both are essential to achieving sustained impact.

The Leadership Equation is about balancing short-term performance with long-term sustainability. Leaders must operate in three time horizons:

- **Short-term**: Managing execution, driving results, solving problems.
- **Mid-term**: Building team capabilities, developing systems, reinforcing strategic alignment.
- **Long-term**: Ensuring purpose alignment, sustaining company culture, growing future leaders, enabling innovation and adaptability.

Leadership Equation

$$\left(\begin{array}{c} \text{Leadership Functions (Results)} \end{array} + \begin{array}{c} \text{Core Leadership Practices}^{™} \text{ (Sustainability)} \end{array} \right) \times \begin{array}{c} \text{Self Awareness (Understanding myself and how others perceive me)} \\ \text{Organizational Support (Purpose, Values, Alignment, Systems, Architecture)} \end{array} = \begin{array}{c} \text{Sustainable Impact on Results (Financial, Culture, Value Creation, Agility)} \end{array}$$

© Working Knowledge Consulting Group, 2010, © The Morphing Group, 2020

Figure II. **The Leadership Equation.** *This model expresses the concept behind sustainable leadership impact. It shows how Leadership Functions (short-term execution) and Core Leadership Practices™ (long-term effectiveness) must be combined and then amplified by Self-Awareness and Organizational Support. Leaders must not only act effectively but reflect intentionally and operate within aligned systems. This equation clarifies what leadership truly demands: execution, behavior, reflection, and the right conditions to thrive.*

But most leaders default to short-term thinking. They focus on hitting targets and solving immediate issues, not because they don't care about the future, but because the company's leadership system prioritizes short-term success over long-term impact.

Anyone who has navigated the complexities of the corporate world knows the familiar refrain: "There's no time for that!" This is the most common response I hear when discussing how companies can address long-term challenges. It's a fallacy—yet a deeply ingrained one. The relentless pressure to meet deadlines, the never-ending cycle of lengthy but ineffective meetings, and the constant urgency of daily priorities leave little bandwidth for leaders to focus on what will happen five or ten years down the road. When survival is measured in quarterly results, long-term thinking feels like a luxury. But this mindset is precisely what creates a self-imposed trap, keeping leaders stuck in the hamster wheel of short-term execution while the future remains an afterthought. If companies want to break this cycle, they must recognize the systems they've built that reinforce it.

Leaders are evaluated on their financial performance, their ability to manage crises, and their operational effectiveness. But rarely are they measured on:

- How many people they have developed into future leaders.
- How effectively they have aligned their team's work with the company's long-term vision.
- Whether they have created a culture of collaboration and trust.

Without these elements, even short-term success becomes unsustainable. Teams burn out, innovation stalls, and leadership pipelines weaken. This is why leadership cannot be defined solely by financial or operational results. It must be defined by the conditions leaders create for sustained success.

Balancing the Leadership Equation

The missing piece in leadership development is awareness. Most leaders do not realize that leadership is a discipline—a set of behaviors that, when executed intentionally, drive long-term success. If there's one variable that silently governs the impact of every leadership action, it's self-awareness. That's why, in this equation, it multiplies the effect. Leadership Functions and Practices may be well-defined, but their effectiveness is filtered through how consciously they are applied. Leaders who lack awareness of their tendencies, triggers, and impact on others often derail performance—not through intention, but through misalignment.

Self-awareness doesn't replace skill—it amplifies or weakens it. And as any leader who has ever misread a situation knows, even the right decision or behavior, poorly delivered, can do damage. In contrast, leaders who act with self-awareness adapt, connect, and lead with intention, elevating the quality and sustainability of their impact. We'll go deeper into this in Chapter 9.

If leadership were just about making the right decisions, knowing more, or working harder than everyone else, companies would not face persistent leadership gaps. In practice, effective leadership has less to do with being the smartest person in the room and everything to do with shaping an environment where great decisions and strong execution happen consistently—even when the leader is not present.

This is where leadership practices come in. They are the mechanisms through which leaders balance short-term execution with long-term sustainability. They are not vague principles or idealistic theories—they are tangible, actionable responsibilities that leaders must execute to ensure their teams, their organizations, and their people thrive beyond immediate results.

Let me pause here to be clear: **Leadership practices are not optional.** They are the job. If you are being paid to lead, then you are being paid to consistently and deliberately execute these practices—extraordinarily well. They are not a complement to your role; they are its very essence.

A company's success is built on its ability to keep growing, evolving, and sustaining results over time. But that only happens if leaders actively create the conditions for it.

If you hold a leadership role, then practicing leadership isn't optional—it's the job.

From Theory to Action: What Leaders Must Do

So, what does this mean in practice? If a leader's responsibility extends beyond execution, what specific actions must they take to fulfill their role?

This is where the three Core Leadership Practices™ come in. They are the answer to the leadership equation—the practical behaviors that bridge the gap between short-term execution and long-term sustainability.

A leader must focus on three fundamental areas:

1. **Providing Clear Direction**—Ensuring alignment, clarity, and purpose so that people know and connect to where they are going and why it matters.
2. **Enabling Capabilities**—Developing, coaching, and equipping people with the tools and confidence to execute and grow.
3. **Activating Value Creation**—Building an environment where people are engaged, motivated, and empowered to contribute their best work and innovate constantly.

Everything a great leader does falls into one of these three practices. They are the blueprint for leadership success—not just in driving results today, but in ensuring the company remains strong and adaptable for the future.

The Core Leadership Practices™ Framework

After years of working with organizations, coaching executive teams, and studying leadership effectiveness, I've learned one fundamental truth: complexity obscures action. Only clear, simple communication enables understanding, application, and lasting impact. That is why the Core Leadership Practices™ approach exists—to cut through the noise and focus on the essentials, as first introduced in **Figure I (Chapter 1)**.

In a world flooded with leadership frameworks, competency models, and vast literature dissecting personality traits and ideal leadership behaviors, it's no surprise that companies fall short in articulating clear, actionable leadership expectations. When leadership development becomes overly complex, it fails to resonate. If leaders cannot grasp what is expected of them in a way that is practical and immediately applicable, meaningful change rarely happens.

I've seen many leadership models built with the right intent—comprehensive frameworks that attempt to reflect the full complexity of what leadership involves. But in trying to cover everything, they often combine too many layers: functions, values, behaviors, styles, and even personality traits. On their own, each element may be valid. But when you're asking leaders to "develop others," "model integrity," "drive results," "foster inclusion," and "be authentic"—all in the same breath—it creates confusion. It becomes unclear what's behavioral, what's cultural, what's stylistic, and what's non-negotiable. The result is that leaders walk away overwhelmed. Instead of clarity, they get a checklist. Instead of direction, they get diffusion. Good intentions aside, when expectations are unclear, execution falters.

That's exactly why the Core Leadership Practices™ focus only on the essential behaviors leaders must execute. Not everything leaders should be: it's what they must do to lead effectively. It may seem almost too simple at first, but that simplicity is precisely what makes it powerful. Time and again, I've seen leaders run into difficulty, not because they lack the capability or the willingness, but because companies overlook how fundamental these practices are to their role.

Figure III provides a visual representation of the Core Leadership Practices™ and the sub-practices that bring each to life. They are specific, observable actions that define how leaders create clarity, enable execution, and activate commitment. While Figure I in Chapter 1 presented the three dimensions of leadership effectiveness, this model focuses specifically on the behavioral dimension and how its components work together to drive sustainable performance.

The model is not mentioned in passing—it forms the spine of this book. In Chapters 5, 6, and 7, each core practice is explored in depth to better understand its meaning, its impact, and the leadership nuances that make it difficult to execute well. These chapters focus on what makes each behavior essential and why mastering this system of action is the key to sustainable leadership effectiveness.

To complete the Leadership Equation and create sustainable impact, improving as a truly effective leader comes down to mastering these three fundamental practices:

1. **Providing Clear Direction**—Ensuring that people understand where they are going, why it matters, and how they contribute. A leader must articulate an attractive and compelling vision of success, establish clear expectations, and define the behaviors that will drive that success. Clear Direction refers not only to the strategic path of the company but also includes the desired culture to create and the direction every team member must aspire to grow toward.

2. **Enabling Capabilities**—Removing obstacles, building team interactions, delegating effectively for growth, coaching, providing meaningful feedback, training, and empowering people to execute and grow. This practice centers on equipping team members with the tools, knowledge, and confidence they need to contribute effectively. Being an arduous endeavor, it also requires patience, insight, time, and intentionality from the leader.

3. **Activating Value Creation**—Building an environment where people are engaged, included, motivated, and aligned toward impact. While motivation is inherently personal, a leader can activate it by connecting with each individual's purpose, celebrating successes, and recognizing progress in meaningful ways. Leaders must pay close attention to their unconscious bias to excel in this practice, and self-awareness and situational adaptability become key.

Most of what great leaders do fall into one of these three leadership practices. They are key to leadership effectiveness, regardless of industry, company culture, or personality type.

Core Leadership Practices™

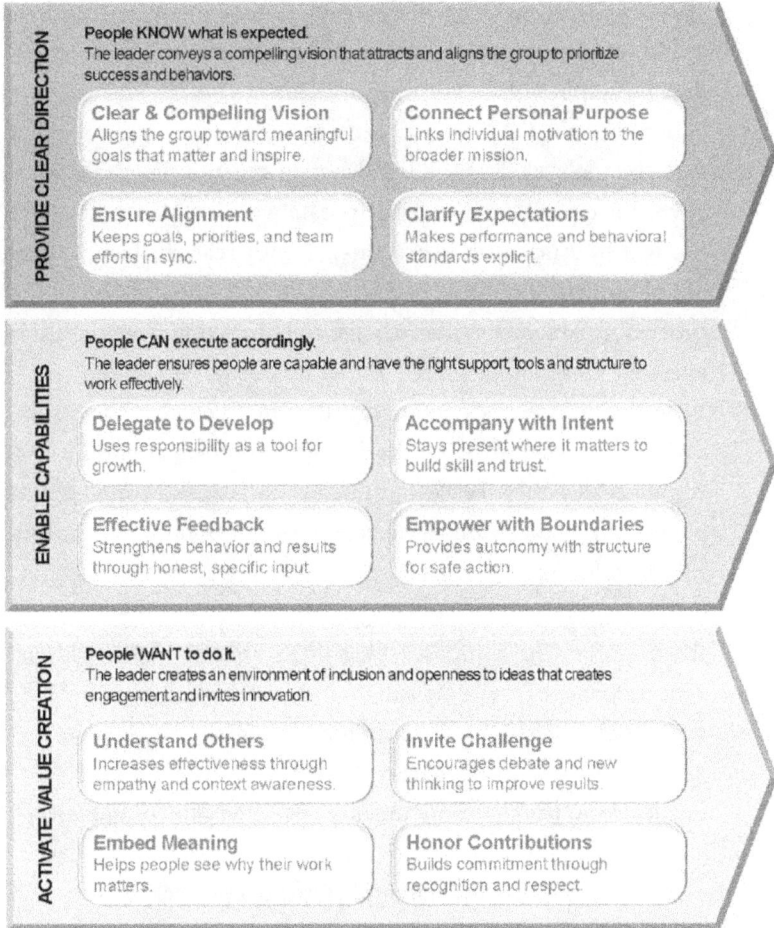

PROVIDE CLEAR DIRECTION

People KNOW what is expected.
The leader conveys a compelling vision that attracts and aligns the group to prioritize success and behaviors.

Clear & Compelling Vision
Aligns the group toward meaningful goals that matter and inspire.

Connect Personal Purpose
Links individual motivation to the broader mission.

Ensure Alignment
Keeps goals, priorities, and team efforts in sync.

Clarify Expectations
Makes performance and behavioral standards explicit.

ENABLE CAPABILITIES

People CAN execute accordingly.
The leader ensures people are capable and have the right support, tools and structure to work effectively.

Delegate to Develop
Uses responsibility as a tool for growth.

Accompany with Intent
Stays present where it matters to build skill and trust.

Effective Feedback
Strengthens behavior and results through honest, specific input.

Empower with Boundaries
Provides autonomy with structure for safe action.

ACTIVATE VALUE CREATION

People WANT to do it.
The leader creates an environment of inclusion and openness to ideas that creates engagement and invites innovation.

Understand Others
Increases effectiveness through empathy and context awareness.

Invite Challenge
Encourages debate and new thinking to improve results.

Embed Meaning
Helps people see why their work matters.

Honor Contributions
Builds commitment through recognition and respect.

© Working Knowledge Consulting Group, 2010 © The Morphing Group, 2020

Figure III. **The Core Leadership Practices™ Framework.** *This model illustrates the three core Leadership Practices—Provide Clear Direction, Enable Capabilities, and Activate Value Creation—along with the specific sub-practices that give each dimension meaning. It aligns each practice with a core leadership responsibility: helping people Know what's expected, ensuring they Can execute, and inspiring them to Want to contribute. Together, these behaviors form the foundation of leadership impact and sustainability.*

A simple way to understand the outcome of these leadership practices is through three foundational conditions for execution: **KNOW**, **CAN**, and **WANT**.

- **When people KNOW** what is expected of them, they are able to focus their efforts, align with the vision, and contribute with clarity and direction. They don't waste time guessing priorities or interpreting vague goals—clarity becomes a catalyst for coordinated action.

- **When people CAN** contribute effectively, they are equipped with the tools, skills, and confidence to execute. They take initiative, solve problems, and collaborate with less dependency on the leader. And as they are trusted with real challenges, they grow through experience, developing new capabilities in the process. Enablement turns passive roles into proactive ones and everyday work into a source of continuous development.

- **When people WANT** to engage, they bring energy, ownership, and discretionary effort to their work. They care about the outcome because they feel seen, valued, included, and connected to a greater purpose. Motivation is no longer a bonus—it becomes a built-in force.

It's important to emphasize that these are not abstract ideals, theoretical concepts, or "soft skills" that can be delegated to HR. These are core leadership responsibilities—tangible, measurable, and directly tied to long-term business success.

Leaders who dismiss these practices as "engagement initiatives" or "nice-to-haves" fail to see the direct impact they have on execution, innovation, and sustainability. A team that lacks clarity will waste time and resources moving in conflicting directions. A team that isn't enabled will be riddled with inefficiencies, bottlenecks, and dependency on the leader for every decision. A team that isn't engaged will deliver the bare minimum, with little ownership or drive.

Yet, many companies still overlook leadership as the active work of ensuring clarity, enablement, and engagement. Because results are often measured in financial or tactical terms, leaders who push for short-term wins without building the infrastructure for sustained success are rewarded—while those who develop people and strengthen teams often go unnoticed.

And so, many leaders assume this isn't their job. They believe developing talent, fostering engagement, and creating alignment are HR's responsibilities. But leadership is the job. Not just hitting numbers, not just managing operations, not just making decisions—but actively building an environment where people can deliver results today and continue to thrive long after the leader is gone.

These are actionable responsibilities, not optional ideals. And they are the difference between a leader who simply holds a position and a leader who actually leads.

The Silent Half of the Job

Let's think about this scenario for a moment: At the end of a long workday, as leaders drive home or close their laptops, how do they measure the success of their day? Most likely, their thoughts follow a familiar pattern: *We hit our sales target. We completed the project. We solved that urgent issue. We made progress on our quarterly goals.*

They evaluate their day based on the functions of leadership—the decisions made, the tasks executed, the crises managed. And while these actions matter, they represent only half of the leadership equation.

How often do leaders reflect on the practices of leadership? How many take a moment to ask themselves:

- *Did I create an environment today where my team felt engaged and energized?*
- *Did I help someone develop a skill that will make them better in the long run?*
- *Did I provide enough clarity for my team to align on what truly matters?*

These questions rarely make it into a leader's end-of-day assessment, yet they define whether success will last beyond today.

Leadership is not just about what gets done—it's about how leaders actively practice the behaviors that drive sustainability. If leaders only measure their success by immediate functional outcomes, they risk neglecting the very practices that will ensure those outcomes continue in the future.

The most effective leaders don't just focus on what they achieved in the short term—they also hold themselves accountable for what they achieved that has a long-term impact. They make it a habit to drive clarity, enable capabilities, and activate their team for value creation. These are not passive qualities; they are actions, just like any other function of leadership. The difference is that while functional actions keep the business moving today, leadership practices ensure it thrives tomorrow.

The key lies in making sure people are clear on the vision (**Know**), equipped to act on it (**Can**), and fully engaged in creating value (**Want**).

The Impact of Poor Leadership Practices

Every dysfunctional team, disengaged employee, or struggling organization I've encountered has suffered because one or more of these leadership practices was missing.

- **When leaders fail to provide clear direction**, teams operate in confusion—people waste time on the wrong priorities, efforts become misaligned, and execution suffers.
- **When leaders fail to enable capabilities**, they create dependency—they micromanage, hoard control, or simply don't develop their teams, leaving them unable to function independently.
- **When leaders fail to activate value creation**, people become disengaged—they do the bare minimum, feel disconnected from their work, and no longer bring their full potential to the table.

Organizations often overcomplicate leadership development, approaching it as a never-ending checklist of skills. In truth, leadership success is driven less by breadth of knowledge and more by the consistent execution of a few critical practices.

The Perception vs. Reality Gap in Leadership Effectiveness

Through my work measuring leadership effectiveness, I've analyzed tens of thousands of data points across different organizations and cultures, looking at how employees assess their leaders. When asked direct questions about their leadership experience—whether they have been clearly explained their role, what is expected of them, and how they can add value (Clear Direction); whether they are being developed, coached, and receiving meaningful feedback (Enablement); and whether they feel recognized, celebrated, and included (Activation)—the responses tend to be mediocre. On average, **29.3% ranked their leader mediocre and 18.5% ranked them low.**[21]

However, we also included a single broad question: "Do you have a good leader?" The response was unexpected. Despite consistently low ratings in specific leadership behaviors, the overall score for this question **jumped by an average of 17 points.**[22]

To understand this gap, we conducted focus groups and leadership interviews, uncovering several key insights:

1. **The Leadership Halo Effect:** Just as organizations find it difficult to define leadership clearly, employees also lack a unified understanding of what good leadership looks like. Many people rate their leader positively not because of actual leadership behaviors but due to personal relationships, communication style,

---

[21] The Morphing Group, *Key Findings on Sustainable Success: 2023 Study on Engagement, Leadership and Flow. Part 1 of 2* (January 2024), https://morphing.guru/resources.
[22] The Morphing Group, internal analysis of aggregated leadership practice data and perception responses across multiple organizations (2023).

or a general "halo effect" that influences their perception. If a leader speaks well, is personable, or is perceived as hardworking, they are often rated favorably—even if their leadership practices are weak or inconsistent.

2. **The Execution-First Mindset:** Many employees don't know what they *should* be receiving from their leaders. When asked about their leaders' role, they most commonly describe execution-based responsibilities—driving results, pushing the team, ensuring efficiency. These are essential leadership functions, but as we discussed in Chapter 1, they are not the full picture. Since leadership practices (such as coaching, developing talent, and fostering engagement) are rarely emphasized in organizations, employees don't expect them—and therefore don't factor them into their assessments.

3. **Bias in Rating a Person vs. Rating a Behavior:** There is a fundamental psychological bias when assessing a specific person versus evaluating specific behaviors. When asked about leadership practices, people are more objective—if they don't receive feedback, they will say so. But when asked about a *person* ("Do you have a good leader?"—whatever their understanding of a "good" leader is), they unconsciously adjust their response, considering personal factors and the challenges their leader may be facing. The ambiguity of the question makes it harder for them to be critical, leading to a more lenient rating.

This is why leadership should not be framed as simply "good" or "bad"—it should be assessed in terms of effective vs. ineffective behaviors. (Don't get me wrong, I do believe bad leaders exist, but for the most part, the issue is that they are simply ineffective.) Leaders are not binary—they exist on a spectrum, with strengths in some areas and gaps in others. Measuring specific practices rather than broad perceptions is key because leadership is always a work in progress. Every leader has areas they excel in and others that need improvement.

One of the most interesting findings from our research was this: If we explained the leadership role to a group of participants *before* they answered the survey—clarifying that leadership is about balancing the Leadership Equation and focusing not just on results but also on key practices—the discrepancy between the leadership practice ratings and the general "good leader" rating **dropped from 17 points to just 3 points.**[23]

This finding has major implications. It suggests that the clearer leadership expectations are at the company level, the leadership level, and the employee level, the more accurately leadership behaviors are recognized and assessed. By defining leadership more explicitly, organizations can:

- Improve leadership selection, ensuring that promotions go to those who embody leadership practices rather than just strong individual contributors.
- Increase accountability, helping leaders understand the behaviors they are expected to demonstrate.
- Enhance leadership development, making it easier to track progress and reinforce the right habits.

In other words, the more intentional companies are in defining and reinforcing leadership, the better they can identify, support, and develop leaders who drive long-term success.

Leadership isn't about arriving—it's about evolving. It's a practice, not a position. One that demands you stay in motion and rise to meet the moment.

[23] Internal research conducted by The Morphing Group in 2022 and 2023 through focus groups and data segmentation. This finding is not included in the public study publication but was observed consistently across pilot sessions.

Leadership Practices vs. Personality

One of the most important insights about leadership is that anyone can develop these practices, regardless of their natural personality. Leadership is not about transforming into a different person—it's about learning how to execute the right behaviors, even if they don't come naturally.

Take Providing Clear Direction, for example. Every leader must ensure their team understands where they are going, why it matters, and how they contribute. But how a leader delivers that clarity will vary:

- A naturally assertive leader may communicate direction in a straightforward, structured manner, setting expectations with clarity and precision.
- A more reflective leader may approach it as a collaborative discussion, gathering input and ensuring buy-in before finalizing the path forward.

Neither approach is inherently better or worse—the measure of success is not the leader's style, but whether the team walks away with a clear understanding of what needs to happen.

The same applies to Enabling Capabilities. Some leaders are natural coaches—they instinctively provide feedback, support, and encouragement. Others may be more inclined to solve problems themselves or focus on execution rather than development. For them, enabling capabilities may require a more intentional effort—learning to step back, create space for team members to take ownership, and offer guidance rather than solutions.

The key is not to change who you are as a person but to recognize which practices may be harder based on your natural tendencies—and then ensure they are still executed effectively. Personality may shape the way leadership practices are delivered, but it should never determine whether they happen at all. The best leaders understand their strengths, identify their blind spots, and commit to developing the practices they need to lead effectively, even if it takes deliberate effort.

What This Means for You

If leadership is a set of practices, then leadership development is no longer about changing who you are—it's about committing to the right behaviors, refining them over time, and making them a habit.

This idea is both liberating and demanding. On one hand, it removes the pressure of needing to fit into a pre-defined mold of what a "great leader" looks like. On the other, it places full responsibility on the leader to be intentional about what they do, rather than relying on who they are.

This is where many leaders go wrong. They assume leadership is innate—that it's all about personality, intelligence, or experience. But these qualities, while helpful, aren't enough on their own. What separates effective leaders is consistent execution.

The reality is this:

- If you are in a leadership role, your effectiveness is not determined by how naturally charismatic, decisive, or experienced you are. It is determined by how well you execute the practices that drive team success.

- If you find any of these areas challenging, that doesn't mean you aren't leadership material—it simply means you have room to improve, just like learning any other skill.

- If you want to become a better leader, the path is clear. You don't have to wait for inspiration, hope that experience will shape you, or rely on instinct. Leadership is not passive—it is active. It is something you do, refine, and improve every day.

The best leaders don't lead based on who they are; they lead based on what they do consistently. And that means that regardless of personality, experience, or natural inclinations, every leader has the potential to be highly effective if they commit to practicing the right behaviors.

Looking Ahead: Understanding Before Mastering the Practices

We've now established that leadership is not about identity, it's about practice. The challenge ahead is about what you do, not who you are. Every leader, regardless of style or background, has the ability to improve by committing to the right actions.

But before diving into leadership practices, there's a crucial step that many overlook—**understanding what makes leadership work in the first place**. The most effective leaders don't just implement techniques; they grasp the deeper dynamics that drive human behavior, decision-making, and engagement.

In the next section, we'll explore the five fundamental principles that amplify leadership effectiveness. These are the foundations that make every leadership practice stronger. Trust, communication, growth, commitment, and engagement are the conditions that determine whether leadership efforts succeed or stall before making real impact.

Mastering leadership isn't just about doing the right things—it's about understanding why they work. And that begins with the fundamentals. Let's dive in.

PART II: LEADERSHIP IN MOTION

Less about identity, more about action

"WE ARE WHAT WE REPEATEDLY DO. EXCELLENCE, THEN, IS NOT AN ACT, BUT A HABIT."
— Aristotle

Chapter 4: Leading Without Understanding? Good Luck with That

Effective Leadership Is About Understanding People, Not Just Implementing Practices

As I've said before, improving as a leader involves developing and applying several key practices. And yes—doing so will absolutely make you better. But if you stop there, you'll miss the real power of leadership. Real effectiveness doesn't come just from executing a formula—it comes from understanding. Specifically, from understanding people. Why they follow. Why they listen. Why they grow, commit, or engage.

Without this understanding, even the best practices will hit a ceiling. They might work, but they won't reach their full potential. And yes, this may sound like more work than you signed up for. But this *is* the work of a leader who wants to do it right. The kind of work that pays off over time because it builds trust, commitment, and impact—making your job not just easier, but more meaningful.

This chapter explores **five fundamental principles** that elevate leadership from mechanical execution to meaningful impact. A leader who blindly applies techniques may get some results—but a leader who starts with understanding unlocks the kind of outcomes that truly shift people and performance.

A leader should focus on understanding the following five fundamental principles for leading people:

- Why would they want to **follow**?
- Why would they want to **listen**?
- Why would they want to **grow**?
- Why would they want to **commit**?
- Why would they want to **engage**?

When you consider that, as a leader, you want people to follow, listen, grow, commit, and engage—not because they're *told* to, but because they *choose* to—it becomes clear: The only way they will is if they truly *want* to. And that means you need to connect with their mindset, beliefs, needs, and aspirations.

1. Why Would People Want to Follow?

(Building Trust)

Trust is the foundation of leadership. Without it, your title doesn't matter. People follow leaders they believe in—leaders who are consistent, fair, and aligned in what they say and do. Trust isn't built overnight, but it can be lost in an instant.

Now, a lot of people in leadership roles have a different idea of what trust means. After all, if you're "the boss," people have to do what you assign, right? Technically, yes. But here's the catch: When people follow because they *have* to, not because they *want* to, they give you the *bare minimum*. They follow instructions—but that's all you get. No insight, no fresh ideas, no proactive thinking. Just task completion.

And that's fine… until something goes wrong. Because when people only do what you tell them to do, guess who owns the result? You do. After all, you gave the order.

Now consider a different scenario—one where your team follows you because they *trust* you. Where they bring their own thinking to the table. Where they offer new perspectives, challenge assumptions, and help you see what you might have missed. That's the real value of trust. It doesn't come from being liked—it comes from unlocking the full intelligence and commitment of the people around you.

When people trust you, they don't just execute your instructions—they help you lead.

Congruence as the Foundation of Trust

As a leader, you are constantly under the spotlight. The company put you in this position for a reason, right? Whether you realize it or not, you are expected to be the embodiment of what the company values. You set the standard, and your actions send an indirect but powerful message about what is permissible, tolerated, and even expected from the rest of the team.

Trust is not an isolated leadership skill—it is the result of being **congruent**. Leaders who say one thing but do another quickly lose credibility. People do not trust titles; they trust alignment between words and actions. A leader may talk about accountability, but if they allow certain team members to avoid consequences, their credibility crumbles. They may advocate for innovation, but if they punish failure, employees will stop taking risks.

Congruence Lives in the Smallest Details

Many years ago, I worked with a retail services client struggling to enforce compliance rules. Leadership was frustrated that employees bent certain policies, arguing for strict accountability.

After one such discussion, I joined the top executive and his advisors in his office. As we sat down, they all lit cigarettes—despite the fact that smoking was recently banned in the building by both company policy and federal law.

I waited until they finished and asked, "Isn't smoking banned here?"

The executive shrugged. "Yeah, but it's just one cigarette."

I leaned back. "That's interesting. So, bending a minor rule is okay for the three of you, but the rest of the team has to follow all the rules exactly?"

What they didn't know was that their employees had already pointed out this hypocrisy. Leaders who demanded strict adherence to rules were the same ones disregarding policies when it suited them.

This is the problem with a lack of congruence. If leaders want to enforce accountability, they can't make exceptions for themselves. Trust isn't built by words—it's reinforced by consistent actions, even in the smallest details.

If you're thinking, *"Well, we no longer smoke at the office,"* you're missing the point. Everything you do—every action, every habit, every small decision—is seen by your team. If you show up late to meetings, take phone calls during a presentation, ignore people in a conference going through your messages, postpone feedback sessions, or criticize other teams instead of working toward solutions, don't be surprised when your people do the same. **Your actions set the standard more than your words ever will**.

Congruence in leadership means that values, decisions, and behaviors align—there is no gap between what is said and what is done. Leaders who don't uphold their own standards breed skepticism and disengagement. Trust erodes when employees experience mixed signals, such as when expectations change without explanation or when commitments are not followed through.

The Three Layers of Trust

Trust is often misunderstood because, like leadership, we tend to treat it as a single concept when, in reality, it has multiple layers. People don't just "trust" a leader—they trust them in different ways and for different reasons. And if any of these layers is weak or missing, trust becomes fragile and incomplete.

The first layer is **Trust in Intent**—the belief that a leader is acting with integrity and good intentions. People need to feel that their leader has their best interests in mind, that they aren't operating with a hidden agenda, and that decisions aren't self-serving or politically motivated. This is the kind of trust that makes people say, *"I may not agree with every decision, but I believe they're doing what they think is best."* Without trust in intent, people question motives, assume manipulation, and start working defensively instead of collaboratively.

Then comes **Trust in Capacity**—the belief that a leader knows what they're doing. You might trust that someone means well, but that doesn't necessarily mean you trust their ability to make sound decisions. A well-intentioned but incompetent leader doesn't inspire confidence; instead, they create hesitation and doubt. People might like them, but they won't follow them in uncertain situations. Capacity trust is what makes people say, *"I trust their judgment. If they say we should move forward, I believe they've thought it through."* Without it, leaders often lack the influence to get buy-in when tough calls need to be made.

And then there's the third layer—**Trust in Vulnerability**. This is the hardest for many leaders, because it means being willing to say, "I don't know," "I made a mistake," or "I need help." We've been conditioned to believe that leaders must always project confidence, certainty, and strength—that admitting uncertainty or a mistake is a sign of weakness. But the opposite is true. People trust leaders who are real. When a leader can acknowledge limitations, seek input, and own their failures, they earn deep, lasting trust. On the other hand, leaders who act like they have all the answers (even when they don't) erode trust, because people can see right through the act.

How Leaders Lose Trust—Often Without Realizing It

Many leaders damage trust unknowingly. A leader who gives unclear direction, constantly shifts priorities, or fails to deliver on promises creates an environment of uncertainty. People start second-guessing decisions, hesitate to take ownership, and disengage—not because they lack motivation, but because they no longer believe in the direction they are being given.

Even small inconsistencies erode trust. Many leaders underestimate how much their behaviors—both big and small—shape how others perceive them. Something as minor as regularly canceling one-on-one meetings, failing to acknowledge contributions, or showing favoritism can have an outsized impact on whether people feel their leader is trustworthy.

Ultimately, trust is not built through grand gestures or motivational speeches. It is built in the smallest, most consistent moments of leadership—when a leader follows through, makes decisions transparently, and models the behaviors they expect from others.

- Trust is **earned through consistency, integrity, and credibility**—not charisma or authority.
- Leaders must be **predictable in values, unpredictable in growth**—you should evolve, but people should always know where you stand.
- **Congruence matters**—your actions, words, and priorities must align.

Use the mirror. Your team is copying your behavior— even the parts you pretend they don't notice

---

2. Why Would People Want to Listen?

(Effective Communication)

People don't listen just because you speak; they listen when what you say connects with what they care about. Effective Communication goes beyond clarity alone—it requires making messages relevant and meaningful.

Communication Isn't About What You Say; It's About What Is Important for Others

One of the biggest mistakes leaders make is assuming that because they said something, people understood it. But communication is not only about transmission; it has a lot to do with reception. Leaders must recognize that a message is only as good as how well it lands with the listener. And every listener is looking out for the same: "What does this message mean for me?"

People don't retain information just because it is clearly stated. They remember what feels *relevant* to them. If a message fails to connect with what matters to the audience, it becomes background noise. A leader who delivers a long-winded speech on company priorities but fails to tie them to the team's daily reality will leave employees nodding but disengaged.

Leaders must ask themselves:
- *Why should my team care about this?*
- *How does this affect them directly?*
- *Am I speaking in a way that resonates with their concerns, aspirations, or challenges?*

If people don't see **why it matters to them**, they won't engage with it.

The Three Stages of Effective Communication

There's a reason we call it *effective* communication—because **it must produce an *effect***. It's not about sounding impressive; it's about whether the message moves people to act. But too many leaders confuse communication with presentation. They think that because they spoke clearly, made a strong case, or delivered a message with charisma, they've done their job. They haven't.

The real job begins with listening.

And not the superficial kind—real listening. Paying attention to nonverbal cues, understanding personalities, decoding what motivates each individual. That's what allows a leader to tailor a message that resonates. You're not just tossing out information—you're crafting a message designed to *create movement*.

You can have the most polished message in the world, but if it doesn't land—if it doesn't get understood, accepted, and acted upon—it missed the mark. And make no mistake: In leadership, failure to communicate effectively isn't just a miss—it creates confusion, disengagement, and misalignment. If your message isn't driving the right effect, then it's just noise.

And when we truly listen and adapt our message, we set the stage for the three essential outcomes of effective communication: understanding, acceptance, and action.

1. **Understanding the Message**—Just because a leader speaks clearly doesn't mean the audience truly grasps the meaning. Messages must be structured in a way that makes them digestible and memorable.

2. **Accepting the Message**—It's not enough for people to hear the message; they need to believe in it. A message is accepted when people see its relevance, value, and alignment with their interests.

3. **Acting on the Message**—The real test of effective communication is whether it has the desired effect. That is when communication drives action. Too many leaders assume their job is done once they've spoken. However, communication is only effective when it leads to clear, purposeful execution.

Step three is where many leaders get tripped up. They assume that if a message was clear and accepted, action will automatically follow. But if people don't know what to do next, the message dies. Great leaders make communication *actionable*—they ensure that people leave with a clear next step.

Be Creative—Effective Communication Is About Purpose, Not Just Words

Some years ago, I worked with a high-performing participant in one of my leadership programs. Sharp, methodical, and assertive, she led a team responsible for auditing internal processes and identifying risks. As a perfectionist, she believed nothing short of flawless execution was acceptable. She reviewed almost every report before it went out—fixing errors, tightening phrasing, and making sure her team didn't slip up.

You could call it micromanagement, and in truth, it was. But the real problem wasn't her need for control—it was that her team didn't share her standards, mostly because she had never truly explained why they mattered. She assumed they would value quality the way she did. They didn't.

That changed during our workshop on communication. She had a realization: "I've been telling them *what* I want, but I've never helped them understand *why* it matters."

Most leaders in her position would double down—issue new rules, maybe give a stern speech about accountability. She did something else.

At her next team meeting, she brought in a box of assorted doughnuts—the colorful kind, with glazes and sprinkles. Just enough for each team member. But before walking into the room, she crushed one of them so badly it looked like someone had stepped on it.

She laid the box on the table and passed around napkins. Everyone grabbed a doughnut, except for the crushed one. When the room settled, she asked, "Why did no one take this one?"

They laughed, shrugged, and said it looked awful. Not appetizing.

And then she made her point: "So, none of you wanted the squashed doughnut because it looked unappealing. You wouldn't want to receive a defective product. So why, then, are you willing to

79

send out half-done, poorly written work to our clients? When you hand in a report with mistakes, or one that hasn't been properly re-searched, it's like serving them this doughnut. You wouldn't want it for yourself—so why would you give it to someone else? And what would you think of the person offering it to you?"

There was silence. And then it clicked.

She went on to name five recurring issues she'd seen in their work—calling each one a "crushed doughnut." They got the mes-sage. No slides, no long speeches, no authority-driven mandates. Just a clear, visual metaphor they could remember.

That team didn't become perfect overnight, but something shifted. They were more careful, more open to feedback, and started owning the quality of their work. And for her, the breakthrough meant she could stop hovering and start trusting. They finally under-stood what she had been trying to say all along.

It's been over a decade, and I still remember the moment she told me that story. Why? Because it proves one thing: Real commu-nication doesn't need complexity—it needs connection. And sometimes, all it takes is a crushed doughnut.

Communication Beyond Words

Leadership communication goes far beyond what's said—it's about what's perceived and what effect it creates. Words are only a small part of the message. Body language, tone of voice, and timing carry just as much weight, sometimes more. You can't say, "I'm open to feedback," and then tense up, get defensive, or shut down the mo-ment someone challenges your view. People pick up on these mixed signals. And when your message and your behavior aren't aligned, credibility suffers.

That's why **listening is as important as speaking**—what we call active listening, not just waiting for your turn to talk. It means paying attention to how people react, not just what they say. Are they engaged, or are their eyes glazing over? Do they seem open and curious, or are they closing down and resisting? Are you speaking to someone who thrives on directness, or someone who needs time to reflect before reacting? You can't connect if you're not paying attention.

People are more likely to listen to you when they feel heard themselves. If you want people to engage with your message, they need to believe that you value their input. Leadership communication is not a broadcast—it's a conversation.

The Role of Framing in Communication

One of the most overlooked aspects of communication is *framing*—how you present the message so it resonates with the person in front of you. You can have the right message, but if it feels like an imposition, not an opportunity, people will resist.

Great leaders understand that how something is said determines how it lands. It's the difference between compliance and engagement. For instance, saying, *"We need to work longer hours to hit this target"* sends one message—more work, more pressure. But reframing that same message as, *"If we pull together now, we'll be in a stronger position for upcoming opportunities,"* changes the tone entirely. The second version speaks to benefit, not burden.

This isn't about sugarcoating reality—it's about making the message matter. People engage when they can connect the task to something meaningful: avoiding future problems, unlocking new possibilities, or stepping into a bigger role. They respond when they see what's in it for them. That's not manipulation—it's simply human nature. Motivation follows meaning.

Common Mistakes Leaders Make When Communicating

Some leaders fall into patterns that weaken their communication without realizing it. For example, they overload people with information. Thinking that more is better, they dump every detail at once—resulting in confusion or shutdown. People process information in chunks. Give them too much, and they retain none of it.

Another mistake is using a one-size-fits-all message. Different people respond to different things—some want data, others want vision. If you speak only in one language, you'll miss part of your team every time.

Leaders also forget to clarify next steps. You can have a great conversation, but if people walk away wondering what they're actually supposed to do, you've missed the mark. Likewise, leaders underestimate the emotional weight of their tone. You might be saying the right things, but if your voice is stressed, cold, or dismissive, the impact will be negative—no matter how solid the content.

And finally, too many leaders fail to read the room. They stay locked into what they want to say, even as it becomes clear the audience is disengaged or confused. The best communicators adjust midstream. They shift tone, reframe, ask questions, or pause to check understanding. Because ultimately, they're not there to deliver a monologue—they're there to create clarity.

Key Takeaways: How Leaders Can Communicate More Effectively

- **Make it about them.** If they don't see why it matters, they won't engage.
- **Ensure clarity, but also relevance.** People process what feels personally important.
- **Frame messages for action.** Communication should inspire clear next steps.
- **Listen first, speak second.** People listen more to leaders who genuinely listen to them.

If they didn't act, maybe they didn't believe. And if they didn't believe, maybe they never really understood why it mattered.

3. Why Would People Want to Grow?

(Development & Learning)

If there's one word every company likes to throw around when talking about people, it's "growth." But as leaders, we need to be honest—what exactly do we mean when we say someone should "grow"? Because growth doesn't look the same to everyone. For some, it means developing new skills. For others, it means moving up the ladder. And for many, it has nothing to do with hierarchy or recognition—it's about doing work that matters, feeling stretched, or being part of something bigger than themselves.

We tend to talk about growth like it's a one-size-fits-all path. But what growth means, and why it matters, is deeply personal. If you want to lead people toward growth, you have to understand what *they* want out of it—not just what you want for them.

Growth Isn't More of the Same—It's Something New

Growth doesn't always happen by doing more of the same. People don't grow just because they've taken on more volume. They grow when they're exposed to new experiences, when they face meaningful challenges, and when they feel a sense of progress—either in capability, confidence, or contribution.

And yet, too often, we confuse repetition with development. We hand someone a longer to-do list, give them a heavier workload, and assume we're "developing" them. That's not a recipe for growth—it's a path to burnout.

Real development happens when people step outside of what they already know. It comes from the stretch—the new project that forces them to think differently, the tough assignment that pushes them out of their comfort zone, or the challenge that awakens a dormant skill.

And most importantly: growth isn't just about gaining skills. It's about gaining clarity, confidence, and purpose.

What Drives People to Want to Grow?

Now, before we get too tactical, we need to pause and ask a deeper question: *Why would someone even want to grow in the first place?*

People don't grow because they're told to. They grow when they *see something in it for them*—when they believe the challenge ahead of them leads somewhere worth going. That's why understanding people's drivers is essential for any leader who wants to foster development. And here's where things get tricky: people are not motivated by the same things.

There are dozens of valid psychological models out there explaining human motivation, and while many are insightful, they often overcomplicate something leaders need to apply in real conversations. So, let's keep it simple.

Based on my experience, there are four broad drivers that consistently show up across different people and situations. They're not the only ones, but they're common enough to give us a practical framework:

- **Social Connection**—Some people grow when they feel connected to others. They thrive in collaborative environments, build energy from teamwork, and feel motivated when they're contributing to something bigger than themselves—together.

- **Mastery & Learning**—Others are driven by the desire to get better. They want to learn, stretch, deepen their craft. These people are at their best when they're constantly being challenged intellectually or technically.

- **Innovation & Impact**—Some are builders and disruptors. They grow through experimentation, solving problems, and creating something new. What drives them is knowing that their ideas can make a difference.

- **Achievement & Progress**—And some are driven by the thrill of winning. They want to move forward, earn recognition, hit milestones, and see tangible signs of progress in what they do.

You might be reading this and thinking, "Well, I relate to more than one of those." That's exactly the point. Most people are moved by more than one driver—and that's good news.

Because it means that when you want to encourage someone's growth, you don't need to pinpoint a single motivation. You just need to *speak in a way that connects with at least one of them*. If someone is motivated by all four, then any one of them might be the spark that pushes them forward.

Growth Has to Be Personal—Or It Won't Stick

This is where leadership makes a difference. If you want someone to grow, don't just assign them a "stretch project" and call it development. Take the time to explain *why* that project matters—not to you, but to *them*.

Frame the opportunity in terms that connect to their drivers:
- "This project will push your skillset into new territory."
- "You'll be working with a new team—it's a great way to build relationships across the business."
- "This is a chance to make a real difference in how we serve our clients."
- "If this goes well, it sets you up for that next role you've been talking about."

When leaders do this well, something shifts. People stop seeing the work as an obligation and start seeing it as a personal opportunity.

This isn't about manipulation. It's about making the purpose of the challenge visible; and from my work in developmental assignments, I have often seen that every project or challenge can offer most of these aspects, the key is to frame them correctly.

A Story of Growth, Potential—and Missed Opportunities

There's someone I met early in her career—sharp, bold, disruptive in the best possible way. She had ideas, challenged assumptions, and clearly wanted to make an impact. Over the years, we've worked together several times, with me in a consulting role. We've kept in touch through her career moves, and aside from considering her a good friend and an extraordinary human being, I see her as a reference, an example of someone who has remained true to her nature. That authenticity is, in my view, the core strength that has driven—and will continue to drive—her growth.

I've also come to know some of her bosses. And depending on who she was working for, I could see it in her eyes—sometimes lit with energy and purpose, other times dulled by constraint. The difference wasn't in her talent or dedication; it was in the space she was given to grow.

She's always been an impactful performer. But today, I believe she's thriving, because she's in a role that lets her lead the way she's wired to. She's driven by impact. Sure, she can deliver results and manage execution, but her brilliance shines when she's encouraged to shape direction, influence thinking, and push her team to new ground.

Some of her past leaders missed that. Maybe they saw her as difficult to "manage." Maybe they felt threatened by her independence. But the cost of not recognizing someone's growth drivers is clear: you get performance, but you miss transformation.

There are leaders who fear high-potential individuals because they challenge the status quo. But if you create an environment that allows them to experiment, supports their disruption, and aligns them with a meaningful vision, they don't just perform—they build legacies.

And yes, these people might outgrow your company. But while they're with you, they leave behind something worth keeping. That's a recipe for real, lasting impact.

If people can't see the point of growing, they won't do it. They'll play it safe, stay in their lane, and miss the kind of development that transforms them—and your business. And for those with high potential who are wired to seek that growth, the alternative is even clearer: They'll leave. They'll go find the environment that gives them the stretch, meaning, and challenge they're not getting from you.

Leaders Must Make Space for Growth

Of course, this also requires that leaders stop hoarding all the good challenges. One of the biggest blockers to team growth is a leader who doesn't delegate the meaningful stuff. If you want people to grow, you must give them something to grow *with*—new problems to solve, authority to make decisions, or responsibilities they haven't held before.

And when they stumble, and they will, you don't punish the learning. You coach it. You debrief. You help them reflect. That's where real growth happens.

Final Thought

Growth isn't a corporate buzzword. It's **a personal, human experience**. And it only happens when people feel like the effort is worth it. As a leader, your role isn't to pressure people into growth—it's to create the conditions where they *want* to stretch.

Because when people want to grow, they do more than change themselves: they transform your organization from the inside out.

Some people aren't hard to lead—they're just too big for the box you put them in.

---

4. Why Would People Want to Commit?

(Ownership, Autonomy, and Purpose)

Commitment and compliance are not the same thing. You can get people to do a job by telling them what to do, monitoring their progress, and holding them accountable. That's compliance. But it's not commitment.

Commitment shows up when people feel ownership—when they believe in what they're doing, have a say in how they do it, and can see how their work connects to something meaningful. And here's the catch: People don't commit just because you ask them to. They commit when they see themselves reflected in the outcome.

Too often, leaders confuse tasks with motivation. They think that if the goals are clear and the deadlines are set, people will throw themselves into the work. But that's just not how most people function. You get from people what you put in them. If you offer them nothing more than a to-do list, they'll check boxes. If you offer them a reason to care, they'll bring more of themselves to the table.

This isn't about soft talk or romanticism. It's not about trying to "inspire" people with empty speeches. In fact, it's about performance. People perform better when they feel part of something that matters—and remember, what "matters" is different for everyone. They put in more effort, stay focused longer, and take more responsibility—because it feels like it's theirs.

Simon Sinek said it well in *Start with Why*—people don't buy into what you do, they buy into why you do it.[24] And that applies just as much to your employees as it does to your customers. If people can see the deeper reason behind the work, they don't need to be pushed. They lean in. Daniel Pink's research in *Drive* reinforces this with three core principles: Autonomy—the chance to own their decisions; Mastery—the chance to grow in something meaningful; and

---

[24] Simon Sinek, *Start with Why: How Great Leaders Inspire Everyone to Take Action* (New York: Portfolio, 2009).

Purpose—the chance to contribute to something greater than themselves.[25]

But if we go a level deeper, we start to understand that real commitment is built when leadership creates the conditions that satisfy four fundamental needs. These aren't just preferences—they're embedded in our nature:

- **Instinctive Needs**—We all need to feel that our basic needs are covered. When people are worried about their income, job stability, health, or even their safety at work, they won't be thinking about innovation or improvement. They'll be in survival mode.

- **Mental Challenge**—People need to feel mentally engaged. They want to grow, explore new ideas, solve problems. Without this, work becomes a repetitive task, and even the most reliable employee can begin to disengage.

- **Emotional Connection**—We are social and emotional beings. People want to feel respected, appreciated, and part of a community. Without this, loyalty fades and performance becomes transactional.

- **Sense of Transcendence**—Once the others are in place, people begin to ask, *What am I contributing to? What bigger story am I part of?* This is where purpose becomes a performance driver—not a slogan.

These four needs are not optional extras. While some people may prioritize one over another, we're all wired to seek them. They form the foundation for deep, lasting commitment. When one is unmet, people hesitate. When several are unmet, they disconnect—emotionally, mentally, or physically.

And yes, there's a risk that if you create this kind of environment—one where high-performing people are trusted, stretched, and valued—they may outgrow your company. But if you've truly

---

[25] Daniel H. Pink, *Drive: The Surprising Truth About What Motivates Us* (New York: Riverhead Books, 2009).

led them well, they'll leave behind a stronger team, a healthier culture, and a legacy of performance. They'll leave something that lasts. That's not a loss. That's leadership done right.

What Leaders Should Do to Foster Commitment

1. **Give up control without giving up direction.**
   Most people don't need to be told what to do every step of the way—but they do need clarity on the destination. Set clear outcomes, then let them choose the best route to get there.

2. **Involve people in defining success.**
   Don't just assign tasks. Invite your team to shape what the work looks like. When they help build the roadmap, they're far more likely to own the journey.

3. **Give autonomy with support.**
   Autonomy doesn't mean abandonment. People need space to decide, but they also need guidance when they ask for it. Be present, but don't micromanage.

4. **Recognize contribution, not just results.**
   When people know their effort is seen, not just their outcomes, they feel respected. Commitment grows when people feel valued, not only for what they deliver, but for what they bring.

5. **Connect decisions to purpose.**
   Every tough call, every shift in priority, every big challenge—tie it back to the "why." Remind people how their efforts matter, not just to the company, but to something they care about.

Let them shape the *how*. Let them understand the *why*. Let them see the impact. People commit when they feel trusted. When they see a piece of themselves in the outcome. When they can say, without being told, *"This matters—and I'm all in."*. **More than idealism, that's leadership.**

> *You'll never get real commitment from someone who feels like a tool for someone else's goal.*

5. Why Would People Want to Engage?

(The Result of Getting Everything Else Right)
Engagement is the holy grail in many leadership conversations. Companies measure it, consultants design programs around it, and HR departments launch campaigns to boost it. But here's a concept that often gets overlooked: Engagement is not something you can directly force. It's the outcome of doing everything else right.

✓ If people trust their leader, they'll follow.

✓ If they feel heard and understood, they'll listen.

✓ If they see opportunities to stretch and grow, they'll take them.

✓ If they feel a sense of ownership, autonomy, and purpose, they'll commit.

And when all of these conditions are present, people engage.

You don't drive engagement by asking for it. You earn it by creating an environment where it can naturally happen.

Too often, companies try to solve "engagement problems" by introducing perks, flexible schedules, or motivational posters. And while some of these tactics might be appreciated, they're superficial if they don't address what really drives people. No free lunch or extra vacation day will compensate for poor leadership, lack of clarity, or an environment where people feel unheard or underutilized.

People engage when the conditions around them make it worth engaging. When they feel challenged, valued, and safe. When they see their work making a difference. When their leaders take the time to understand them—not just manage their output.

You can't force engagement, but you can create the conditions for it:

• If you want people to care, make the work meaningful.

• If you want people to go beyond their role, trust them with real responsibility.

• If you want people to show up fully, give them something to show up for.

Engagement doesn't begin with an employee. It begins with leadership.

And it begins with understanding.

What Leaders Should Remember About Engagement

- **Engagement is not a tactic—it's a result.** If you chase engagement without building trust, purpose, growth, and ownership, you'll always fall short.
- **People engage differently.** Some are fueled by connection, others by challenge, some by autonomy, others by impact. Knowing your team is not optional—it's leadership.
- **Engagement requires consistency.** You can't give clarity one week and disappear the next. You can't empower people once and then micromanage them later. People stay engaged when the environment stays reliable.
- **Engagement is fragile.** It can take months to build and minutes to destroy. That's why leaders must be intentional, not reactive. Every conversation, decision, and behavior sends a signal.

Getting It Wrong: Why Most Engagement Measurements Mislead

Before closing this fundamental, I want to offer a caution that comes from years of working on engagement measurement and studying models across the industry.

There's a big business around measuring and fostering engagement (tools, workshops, benchmarks, platforms) but many of them miss a critical distinction: they confuse satisfaction with relevance. Companies often celebrate survey results that show high satisfaction with compensation, environment, or leadership style, assuming they've "won" at engagement.

But satisfaction alone doesn't drive engagement. Relevance does.

People aren't driven just because they're satisfied with a factor—they're driven when the things they care *most* about are being fulfilled. You might be satisfied with your salary, but if your need to grow, to belong, or to create impact isn't being met, you won't feel truly engaged.

Unless your measurement model tells you the difference between what's "nice to have" and what's *personally meaningful,* leaders will draw the wrong conclusions. That's a deeper topic I won't fully unpack here, but it's something I've explored extensively in my work around organizational flow and engagement. For now, the takeaway is simple:

Engagement isn't about feeling good. It's about feeling so fulfilled and aligned that you are compelled to add value.

And both fulfillment and alignment only happen when what matters to the company overlaps with what matters to the individual.

And that's why we end here.

Because when people engage, they bring more than their skills. They bring their attention, creativity, energy, and drive. They stop being passengers and start becoming owners. And when that happens, leadership becomes something more than direction—it becomes momentum.

This fifth fundamental doesn't just close the list.

It completes it.

People don't engage because you said the right words. They engage because you built the right conditions.

Looking Ahead: Leadership Begins with Understanding People

These five fundamentals are the foundation on which effective leadership is built. You can apply all the right practices, follow every framework, and manage every task with precision, but if you don't understand why people follow, listen, grow, commit, and engage, you'll never move people—only processes.

When you start with understanding, everything changes. Leadership becomes less about controlling outcomes and more about enabling people. It shifts from a role you play to a responsibility you embody.

That's the difference between managing tasks and leading people.

The chapters that follow will go deeper into specific leadership practices, beginning with how leaders provide **Clear Direction**. Now that you understand the "why" behind people's behavior, it's time to explore the "how"—how leaders create clarity not just in words, but in action. Because once people understand *why* something matters, your job is to help them understand exactly *what* they're supposed to do, and *how* they can succeed. Ready to dive in?

Before You Begin the Practices

What follows is not a set of leadership tips, it's a framework for practicing leadership in a way that outlasts you. These practices are clear by design. Leaders usually don't fail for lack of knowledge; they fail for lack of clarity, conviction, or consistency. Let's be honest: Knowing what matters is not the same as doing it.

This section is here to show you what leadership looks like when it's built to last, not to pretend that implementation is linear or easy. You will see yourself in these pages, sometimes with pride, sometimes with discomfort. And that's exactly the point. Because the moment you recognize yourself is the moment the real work begins.

Chapter 5: The Practices of Providing Clear Direction

The Leadership Discipline That Cannot Be Delegated

If there is one job that a leader cannot outsource, avoid, or ignore, it is Providing Clear Direction. Vision, alignment, and execution all depend on it. Without clarity, even the most capable team can get off track. Resources get misallocated. Priorities compete. Initiatives stall. People default to local optimization rather than collective advancement. In this vacuum of clarity, frustration grows, trust erodes, and engagement declines.

It is common for leaders to assume they are being clear because they have stated the strategy, shared the objectives, or repeated the vision. But clarity doesn't reside in what the leader *says*—it lives in what people *understand, accept,* and *act upon.*

As discussed in Chapter 4, the goal of communication isn't eloquence, it's impact. And that impact is clarity. Not theoretical, not rhetorical—operational. Real clarity means every person understands what matters, why it matters, and what to do about it.

More importantly, clarity requires congruence. When people trust their leader's intentions, competence, and vulnerability, they are more likely to accept direction and align behind it. But clarity doesn't end with trust. It needs structure to become sustainable. And this is

something many leaders misunderstand: They communicate messages without ensuring the organization is designed to support them.

How many times have you, as a leader, tried to convey a clear
message—only to realize that internal processes, conflicting priorities, or the reward system are pulling in a different direction? That's
what I mean by organizational alignment: the structure that either
supports or undermines the clarity you're trying to create. And more
often than not, even at the highest levels, I find that this structure
isn't discussed thoroughly enough to truly support leadership direction.

Clarity Requires Structure: The 7 Factors of Organizational Effectiveness

To lead with clarity, good intentions and powerful speeches are not
enough. Leaders must provide direction within a coherent system.
Without structural alignment, direction becomes noise. Leaders start
giving mixed messages, priorities shift constantly, and execution becomes inconsistent.

This is why Clear Direction must be anchored in a broader
framework. One that connects vision to execution. One that helps
people understand how the organization works and where their role
fits.

If you've ever found yourself communicating one thing while
the system reinforces another, you're not alone. This tension between what leaders say and what the organization signals through its
processes is where clarity often breaks down. That's why we need
more than a strong message—we need a structure that helps people
make sense of it. That's where alignment becomes essential. And to
make direction sustainable, we need a framework that connects leadership intention with how the business actually works.

The **Seven Factors of Organizational Effectiveness™,**
shown in **Figure IV,** work as an integrated system. When aligned,
they create an environment where teams execute seamlessly. When

misaligned, they create friction, inefficiency, and confusion—and that's where leadership effectiveness is most at risk.

This model was first developed in 2010, when I founded and led Working Knowledge Consulting Group. It has since evolved through years of consulting work across industries and now remains a foundational methodology of **The Morphing Group**. What makes it powerful is not only its simplicity, but its ability to help leaders ask the right questions in the right order.

What follows is a high-level overview meant to introduce the logic of the model—not an exhaustive breakdown of each component. Each factor could warrant deeper exploration, but for now, the goal is to establish a shared understanding of how they interact and why structural clarity matters.

In today's fast-changing environment—marked by disruption, reinvention, and shifting stakeholder expectations—it doesn't matter whether you're a global corporation or a startup in a garage, whether your structure is hierarchical or tribal, nimble or robust. Every organization, regardless of size or industry, depends on these seven factors to operate effectively. They are universal requirements for coherence and impact. At the core of them all is Purpose—a force that gives aspirational meaning to what the company does. It has always mattered, but now more than ever, a clearly articulated purpose positions organizations to influence not just shareholders, but also customers, employees, and the broader world they serve.

Let's take a closer look at each factor and why clarity is essential in making them work.

True clarity is not what a leader declares—it's what the organization reinforces in silence.

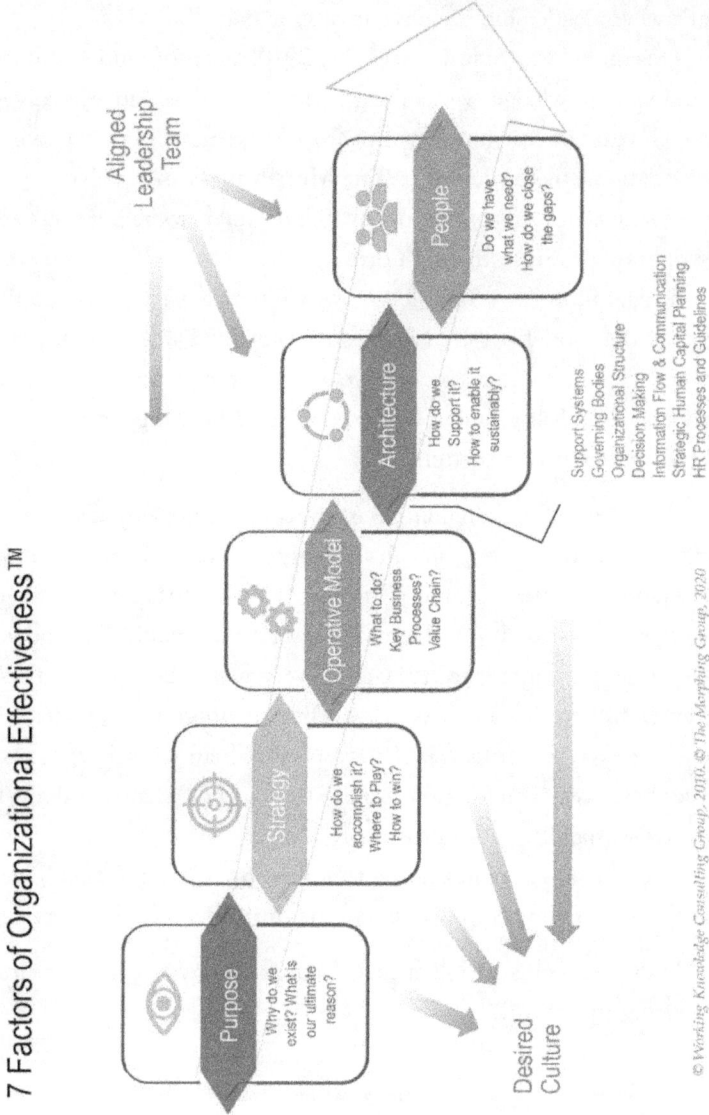

Figure IV. **The 7 Factors of Organizational Effectiveness™** - *Sustainable performance emerges when Purpose, Strategy, Operating Model, Organizational Architecture, People, Leadership, and Culture are aligned and reinforced. Leadership acts as the catalyst that ensures this alignment drives results and resilience over time.*

Purpose: The Foundation of Alignment

Every organization exists for a reason, and Purpose is the starting point. It defines why the company exists beyond making money, shaping its identity, values, and long-term ambition. A clear and effective purpose isn't just a statement on a website—it's a compass that should guide decision-making and priorities.

Leaders who don't convey a clear purpose create organizations that drift, reactively chasing short-term wins instead of building something sustainable. Without a well-defined purpose—and a leader who ensures everyone understands how it connects to their daily work— employees are less likely to understand why their contributions matter, and misalignment spreads.

Strategy: The Roadmap to Execution

If purpose defines *why* we exist, strategy defines *how* we achieve it. The essence of strategy lies in making clear choices—where to play, how to win—not in doing everything well. Companies often underperform not from lack of effort, but from lack of focus.

But strategy is not just about financial goals, sales targets, or competitive positioning. If the company's purpose speaks to improving the lives of clients, fostering innovation, or creating a positive environment, then strategy must also address how those outcomes will be achieved. Yet, in practice, strategy documents often focus solely on short-term metrics and ignore how the company intends to deliver on its stated purpose. This creates a disconnect between what the company claims to stand for and what it actually prioritizes. Every factor in the organizational system must align with the one before it—so strategy must include how we will create value for clients, support our people, contribute to society, and, of course, deliver results.

When leaders don't provide clarity in strategy, employees either pull in different directions or work on tasks that don't contribute to the company's success. A good strategy prioritizes what matters most and provides a roadmap that aligns all efforts toward a common goal.

Operating Model: How Value Is Delivered

The Operating Model defines how the company creates and delivers value. It consists of business processes, workflows, and cross-functional interactions that allow the company to function efficiently. If strategy is the *how*, the operating model is the *what*—the system that ensures that work flows properly, that departments collaborate effectively, and that the value chain is structured for efficiency.

When operating models lack clarity, execution slows down. Bottlenecks appear, duplication of efforts increases, and teams lose sight of how their work connects to the broader system. It is the leader's responsibility to define how different parts of the company should interact, clarify key business processes, and intervene when operational inefficiencies get in the way. Leaders must not only understand the operating model—they must communicate it clearly and shape it to enable execution.

Organizational Architecture: The Infrastructure for Success

While the operating model defines how work flows, Organizational Architecture determines how the company is structured to support execution. It includes governance mechanisms, decision-making processes, the flow of information, and all human capital practices—including hiring, performance management, compensation, succession planning, and career development.

This factor is often misunderstood. Many organizations invest heavily in architecture—especially in HR programs—but neglect to align them with the preceding factors: purpose, strategy, and operating model. It's common to find companies with advanced talent development initiatives, competency models, or performance systems that still fall short on execution. Why? Because the architecture was built in isolation. When these systems don't reinforce strategy or reflect how the organization actually operates, they create friction rather than enablement.

Moreover, the lower we go on the 7 Factors, the more critical leadership congruence becomes. No matter how well-designed a talent process is, it will fail if leaders don't understand their role in making it work. Performance management, feedback cycles, and career development all depend on whether leaders apply them consistently, credibly, and in alignment with company goals. Misalignment is one problem—lack of leadership ownership is another. Effective architecture only functions when leaders bring it to life.

People: Having the Right Talent in Place

The People factor isn't about systems—it's about the human beings inside them. While HR processes belong to the Architecture, this factor focuses on whether the organization has the right people in place, and whether those individuals are enabled, motivated, and aligned. It asks three essential questions:

- Based on everything else—our purpose, strategy, operating model, and architecture—**what kind of talent do we require** (not only today, but for where we are headed)?
- **Do we already have that talent inside the organization**—or is it accessible externally?
- And **if there is a gap, how do we close it**—through hiring, development, or reallocation?

A company may have a sound strategy and a well-designed structure, but without the right people, execution falters. Leaders must constantly assess whether the capabilities, experience, and mindset in the organization are sufficient—and act when they're not

Leadership: The Catalyst for Alignment

Leadership is not just another factor—it is the force that activates all the others. Even the most well-designed strategy, processes, and governance systems will collapse without effective, aligned leadership. Leaders provide the energy, clarity, and consistency that turn an organizational framework into action.

Leadership clarity here means ensuring that leaders at all levels understand their role in reinforcing strategy, modeling behaviors, and keeping teams aligned. A misaligned leadership team creates conflicting priorities, inconsistent execution, and organizational drift.

Culture: The Reflection of Everything Above

Culture is not something the company or its leaders declare—it is the natural result of how the company operates. It is shaped by purpose, strategy, decision-making, leadership behaviors, and people practices. If any of these factors are misaligned, the culture that emerges will not be the one the company intended.

Leaders must be clear about the culture they want to reinforce—not just through words, but through daily actions, decision-making, and how they hold people accountable. Culture, when aligned, becomes a powerful force that drives engagement, execution, and long-term success.

Each of the leadership practices we will now explore sits within this structure. Without it, these practices will be temporary fixes. Within it, they become powerful enablers of execution.

Let us now examine the four practices that bring Providing Clear Direction to life and explore how each one supports the five fundamentals of human understanding we discussed in the previous chapter. What makes people want to Follow, Listen, Grow, Commit, and Engage? These aren't just communication goals; they are the filters through which people process, believe, and act on direction.

An organization without alignment is like a symphony without a score—everyone plays, but no one creates music.

Practice 1: Provide a Clear and Compelling Vision

People don't follow spreadsheets—they follow meaning. But meaning doesn't emerge from slogans or speeches—it comes from clarity with emotional weight. A compelling vision is not about hype. It is about helping people see where we are going, why it matters, and what success looks like—*in a way that makes them care.*

A common misstep is stopping at abstraction—mistaking vague ambition for real direction. Some leaders think they're being visionary when they're just being vague. "We want to be the best in our industry." "We will disrupt the market." "We aim to grow sustainably." These statements don't move people. They don't clarify anything. They might sound strategic, but they're too generic to matter.

Clarity isn't about wordsmithing—it's about **intentionality**. It's about the leader making a personal and strategic choice: *This is where we're going. This is what we will fight for. This is how we'll know we're winning.*

But let's go deeper. Can you, as a leader, articulate your vision in a way that passes three essential filters?

- **Where are we going?** (Not directionless ambition—what specific future are you pointing toward?)
- **Why does it matter?** (Why now? Why to us? Why to our clients, partners, or the world?)
- **What does success look like?** (What outcomes signal that we've made real progress?)

Answering these questions is not enough. The challenge is to make the answers meaningful to *people who are different from you.* Your team doesn't all think alike. Some are driven by big-picture purpose. Others want to solve complex problems. Some seek influence, recognition, or the chance to grow. A compelling vision accounts for this spectrum—it offers multiple points of connection.

The goal is not to dilute the message but to broaden its relevance. One vision. Many doors in.

If your vision only appeals to one kind of person, it will only mobilize a fraction of your organization. A well-crafted vision speaks to the ambitious and the cautious, the idealists and the pragmatists. It allows each person to imagine themselves succeeding within it— not just following it but finding meaning in it.

This is what turns direction into motivation. Without this connection, you'll get compliance, not commitment.

And here is the part many leaders forget: A compelling vision isn't just stated—it's shared, reinforced, and retranslated. Too frequently, leaders treat the articulation of a vision as the finish line, when it's only the start. But real impact happens later: in meetings, in conversations, in how managers translate the message to their teams.

If the receptionist at your headquarters doesn't understand how her work contributes to the larger vision—you haven't finished the job. If your frontline supervisor can't explain how today's shift moves the company forward, clarity hasn't landed.

The true art of vision isn't just in its creation—it's in its connection. That's what separates high-concept leaders from high-impact ones.

Questions Leaders Should Ask Themselves:

- If I asked ten people in my team what our vision is, would they give me the same answer?
- Does our vision feel relevant to what we're doing today—or does it live in a future no one recognizes?
- Am I communicating vision, or just repeating slogans?
- Have I made space for different personalities to see something valuable in the path ahead?

Why This Practice Matters Through the Lens of Human Understanding

A vision isn't compelling just because it's clear to you—it's compelling when others get it, accept it, and act on it. And that requires more than just articulation—it requires empathy.

- **A compelling vision makes sense the first time someone hears it**—no slide deck required. If they need a presentation file to explain it, it's too complicated. Ask yourself: *Would this make sense to someone new on the team on their first week?*

- **Understanding isn't the same as believing**. People must see the relevance, the meaning. It has to connect to something they care about—whether that's impact, recognition, stability, growth, or purpose. *Does this vision make people feel part of something that matters?*

- **Even the most inspiring vision means nothing if it doesn't guide behavior.** If your people believe in it but don't know what they're supposed to do differently—then clarity hasn't been achieved. *Does your vision make next steps obvious?*

Clarity of vision isn't about slogans—it's about how deeply people believe in the future you describe. If that vision doesn't feel real, personal, or repeatable, it will never take hold. Your job is to make it tangible, help others see themselves inside it, and repeat it until it shapes behavior.

The challenge isn't creating the vision—it's living it consistently, and making it clear enough that others can carry it without you. Ask yourself: If you stopped talking about it tomorrow, would the story survive?

Practice 2: Connect Direction to Personal Purpose

A clear and compelling vision opens the door. But it's not enough to get people in. To move forward with commitment, people need to see how the vision connects to *them*—their role, their identity, their aspirations. Without that link, even the best vision stays abstract. It might inspire from a distance, but it won't activate ownership.

It's easy to overlook the second step—translating vision into personal relevance. Many leaders assume that sharing the destination is enough. After all, *we're here to do a job*, right? True—but if people can't see how they fit into that journey, how their contributions matter, or what's in it for them, they won't engage with full intent.

If you're expecting added value, innovation, overperformance, or people going the extra mile, there has to be something *they* are striving for—something that connects the company's direction to a personal goal or motivation.

You'll hear the disconnect in the language:

- "I do my job. What else do they want from me?"
- "I know where we're headed, but I don't know what I am supposed to bring to it."
- "I understand the company's vision, I just don't see myself in it for the long-term."

Great leaders bridge this gap. They make the vision personal.

That doesn't mean creating a custom narrative for every employee. It means understanding what drives different people—and deliberately connecting the direction of the company to the values, ambitions, and energy of the individuals within it.

Some people find purpose in building something meaningful. Others want to grow, to prove themselves, or to gain recognition. Others want to solve problems no one else can. When a leader knows what fuels each person, they can connect that energy to the broader direction—and in doing so, unlock real commitment.

This isn't soft leadership—it's precise alignment. When direction connects to purpose, people don't just comply—they invest. And it's not enough to do this well with your direct reports. You also need to teach them how to cascade this approach with their teams. That's the only way to reach the full depth of the organization and make purpose-driven alignment scalable.

Questions Leaders Should Ask Themselves:

- Do I know what drives the people on my team, beyond their job descriptions?
- Have I had real conversations about what success means to them?
- Have I explained how their personal growth fits within the direction we're pursuing?
- When people seem disengaged, do I assume they don't care—or ask if they've lost the connection?

Why This Practice Matters Through the Lens of Human Understanding

Understanding and accepting direction is not just a cognitive exercise—it's also an emotional one. People don't fully commit their energy to a purpose they don't genuinely feel. If leaders want their teams to fully embrace the company's direction, they must show how it aligns with each person's internal compass.

When a person feels that their daily work contributes to something that reflects who they are—or who they want to become—that's when engagement turns into commitment. This connection deepens trust and fuels action. But it doesn't happen automatically. Leaders must create the space for these conversations and lead them with intent.

- **People need to see that the direction aligns with their values, interests, or ambitions**. That's what makes it matter. A leader gives clear direction when they take the time to explore any dissonance or lack of alignment that team members might be experiencing. It takes time—but it's an effort that pays off.
- In this process, **when leaders show that they understand and care about what drives their people, they build credibility**—and belief in the journey ahead. It helps both the individual and the team when everyone is bought into the direction being set.
- **When someone sees how their role fits into something they care about, motivation becomes self-sustaining**. Motivation, as we've explained, is intrinsic—it must come from the person. And it requires reflection and investment to guide people toward understanding this connection and building trust in it.

Motivation is not static—and it's rarely obvious. What moves someone today might not be what moved them last year. Your role as a leader is to keep seeing the person beneath the role and to connect their drive with the direction of the organization. That doesn't mean tailoring work to individual preferences—it means finding alignment worth committing to. The real question isn't whether people are motivated—it's whether you're paying close enough attention to see what's motivating them now.

Practice 3: Ensure Alignment and Understanding with Strategy

Strategy, by definition, is choice. It sets direction by deciding where to focus, what to ignore, and how to win. But too often, strategy is communicated as a collection of priorities, initiatives, and metrics—without clarity on what it all means for people's day-to-day decisions.

Leaders assume that once strategy is announced, it is understood. But strategy isn't understood until it's operational. If teams don't know how to act on it, make decisions through it, or adjust their priorities because of it—then it's still just theory.

This is where many leadership teams lose traction. The message is delivered, the slides are shared—but the translation never happens. And when people don't understand how strategy connects to their work, they either over-index on what they've always done or create their own interpretation. Both lead to drift.

A strategy that isn't translated becomes theater. It might impress in a presentation, but it leaves teams guessing.

A leader's job is to bridge the gap between strategy as a concept and strategy as behavior. That means translating it:

- Into language people understand.
- Into priorities they can act on.
- Into decisions they know how to make.

The 7 Factors model becomes especially useful here: It acts as a diagnostic to spot where alignment is breaking down. If the strategy points in one direction, but the operating model still supports legacy processes... if the architecture rewards different behaviors... if the wrong people are in critical roles—then strategic clarity is compromised. And once clarity breaks down, execution unravels.

Questions Leaders Should Ask Themselves:

- Have I made the strategy actionable at every level, or just understandable in concept?
- Can my team explain how their work advances our strategic priorities?
- Are our systems—governance, recognition, resource allocation—reinforcing the strategy or working against it?
- Do I revisit the strategy often enough for it to stay relevant in people's minds?

In today's world, creating fluid environments is no longer optional. Strategies are constantly confronted by shifting contexts—

new technologies, demographic changes, economic pressures, and global disruptions. To stay effective, leaders must develop the habit of continuously checking for understanding and alignment.

Strategy must be flexible, agile, and anchored in dialogue. Every significant context shift—whether it's a competitor's move, a legislative change, a market disruption, or a global crisis—should prompt a review of the 7 Factors. Ask yourself: *Does this alter our strategy? Our operating model? Our talent needs?* It's not a one-time exercise. It's the ongoing job of leadership: staying aligned in motion.

So don't just ask these questions—build the discipline to revisit them regularly, with the intention of keeping your organization in forward movement.

Why This Practice Matters Through the Lens of Human Understanding

People don't align with strategy because it's elegant—they align with it when it becomes usable.

- **Strategy must be communicated in a way that breaks down complexity and clarifies intent**. If people are left guessing what matters most, they won't guess well.
- **When strategic direction is reinforced by consistent decisions and actions, people start to believe in it—and act with confidence**. This is why congruence and aligned messages are critical: People tend to disconnect from strategy when what they see is different from what they hear.
- **Strategy isn't one message—it's many conversations**. The more it shows up in priorities, feedback, and resource decisions, the more it becomes real. As often as possible, leaders should frame every message, decision, or instruction by linking it to the long-term strategy—making sure everyone understands how the required actions fit into the big picture.

Strategic alignment doesn't come from repetition—it comes from relevance. People follow strategy when they can see how it connects to their role, their decisions, and their success. But alignment isn't imposed—it's built through dialogue, modeling, and structural consistency. If your systems say one thing and your strategy says another, people will believe the system. Clarity is a pattern, not a presentation.

Practice 4: Clarify Expectations–Goals, Priorities, and Behaviors

Even with a clear vision, strong connection to purpose, and a well-translated strategy—execution will still fall apart without clarity in expectations. People cannot act with focus or urgency if they're unsure what success looks like, what's most important, or how they're expected to behave along the way.

Expectations are not just about assigning tasks. They're about setting shared standards for outcomes, priorities, and conduct. And the absence of this clarity breeds two equally dangerous dynamics: chaos or disengagement. A vague leader fosters confusion and inconsistent effort. An overly rigid leader may crush initiative and trust. But a leader who clarifies, adapts, and reinforces expectations consistently creates the conditions for ownership, alignment, and performance.

At the heart of this practice is leadership presence. It doesn't mean micromanaging—it means staying close enough to define direction, while remaining far-sighted enough to anticipate what could get in the way.

Many newly appointed leaders don't fully grasp this distinction—and I'd say many experienced ones don't either. When you know what needs to be done and how you expect people to behave, it's easy to assume that everyone else sees it the same way. That assumption leads to frustration on both sides. But I've seen time and again that clarifying conversations pay off quickly. Most people want to do a good job. Taking the time to understand someone's rationale, decision-making process, or work style often reveals that the problem isn't performance—it's misalignment.

When expectations are clear:

- People make faster, better decisions.
- Teams move with greater autonomy and less friction.
- Leaders don't waste time on rework, misalignment, or silent resistance.

Clarity, here, is not a one-time conversation—it's a discipline.

In today's world, where hybrid and remote work are increasingly common—and still the subject of debate—this practice becomes even more critical. People in the office can be just as disengaged as people working from home. The issue isn't location—it's the absence of clear expectations.

This isn't an argument *for* remote or hybrid work. It's a reminder that the real challenge isn't performance by default—it's the need for stronger, more intentional leadership. Remote work does bring disadvantages, especially when it comes to building engagement, fostering collaboration, or sustaining team dynamics. We do lose part of the informal connection that happens naturally in person—and that needs to be assessed. But the idea that remote work inevitably leads to lower performance has been widely debunked by research and real-world results.[26] In fact, it often reveals where leadership practices fall short—because the need for clarity, feedback, and direction becomes far more visible.

When leaders create clarity in goals, standards, and behaviors, and consistently acknowledge progress, geography becomes irrelevant. People can be across the world and still perform exceptionally well.

---

[26] Nicholas Bloom et al., "Does Working from Home Work? Evidence from a Chinese Experiment," *Quarterly Journal of Economics* 130, no. 1 (2015): 165–218; José Maria Barrero, Nicholas Bloom, and Steven J. Davis, "Why Working from Home Will Stick," *NBER Working Paper* No. 28731 (April 2021), https://www.nber.org/papers/w28731.

It's a form of leadership laziness to insist on physical presence just to make sure people "work," as if being in an office from 9 to 5 guarantees attention or effort. People's minds wander—regardless of where their bodies are. A leader who gives clear direction, defines milestones, links them to strategy in a practical and transparent way, and maintains ongoing clarity in expectations will be effective no matter where their team sits.

Questions Leaders Should Ask Themselves:

- Have I explicitly communicated what success looks like—not just in metrics, but in behaviors?
- Do people know what to prioritize when trade-offs arise?
- Are my expectations visible in the way I give feedback, recognize effort, or intervene?
- Is my team clear on what is *non-negotiable* versus what can flex based on context?

Why This Practice Matters Through the Lens of Human Understanding

When people are unclear about expectations, they default to self-preservation, not initiative. They hesitate. They cover themselves. They do the minimum—not because they don't care, but because they don't want to get it wrong.

- **Clarity gives people permission to move**. When expectations are visible, aligned, and consistently reinforced, it removes second-guessing and unlocks initiative. Some leaders avoid this discipline because they fear it takes too much time. But over time, clarity creates a more fluid environment—where agility and performance emerge more naturally.
- **Expectations aren't a one-time memo**. They must be modeled, repeated, and corrected in real time. For both expected and unexpected behaviors, leadership presence means being alert and responsive. A quick, respectful comment after strong (or poor) performance in a meeting can go a long way. Your role is

to continuously send clear signals—"This is what we need more of," or "This isn't aligned with our purpose or strategy"—and explain the reasoning behind it.

- **People rely on consistent signals**. When expectations are applied fairly and transparently, trust grows—not just in the system, but in you as their leader. This is where congruence becomes non-negotiable. If you expect a behavior, you must model it. Nothing erodes trust faster than a leader who reinforces a standard they don't uphold themselves.

People don't rise to vague expectations. If you want clarity, define success—and then make it visible in the way you coach, give feedback, and make decisions. It's not just about what to aim for, but about how to get there, and how to correct course when things drift. The real challenge isn't setting expectations—it's sustaining them, especially when results are good but behaviors are off. That's when leadership gets tested.

And remember: Your silence sets the standard. Every time you tolerate misalignment, postpone a hard conversation, or reward outcomes that contradict your values, you reinforce confusion. Expectation-setting is not a one-time declaration—it's a pattern you create, one interaction at a time.

Clarity ends not when people can repeat your message, but when they can embody it without needing your voice in the room. That's when direction becomes theirs—and leadership becomes scalable.

Clarity doesn't scale on its own. It's a leader's job to connect the message, align the system, and make expectations unmistakable.

Looking Ahead: Providing Clear Direction Is a System, Not a Speech

As I have been pointing out, Providing Clear Direction is not a communication event. It is a system of leadership behaviors and organizational alignment. It begins with trust, is sustained by structure, and is reinforced through daily leadership discipline.

When people know what matters, why it matters, and what is expected of them—and when the organization is designed to support that understanding—clarity moves from aspiration to execution.

Providing Clear Direction takes shape through four practices:

- **Providing a compelling vision** that speaks to both purpose and emotion.
- **Connecting direction to personal purpose** so people see where they fit.
- **Ensuring strategic alignment** so the message becomes behavior.
- **Clarifying expectations** so execution becomes consistent and empowered.

These practices work together—not in isolation—and they must be reinforced continuously, not just declared. Clarity is a leadership discipline, not a communication style.

Once people are clear on where they're going and what's expected (they *know*), the next question becomes: **Do they have what they need to get there?** (they *can*).

In the next chapter, we move from direction to **capability**—from setting the path to equipping people to walk it with skill and confidence.

Chapter 6: The Practices of Enabling Capabilities

Before diving into the practice itself, it's important to understand where this chapter sits within the broader leadership journey we've been constructing.

In the previous chapter, we focused on Providing Clear Direction—the first and foundational leadership practice. Clarity is not optional. Without it, no team can really align, no strategy can be effectively executed, and no leader can expect true high performance. But clarity is not the finish line—it's the starting point.

Once clarity is established, and once the organizational context is aligned through the 7 Factors of Organizational Effectiveness™, a new responsibility emerges: ensuring that the system you've built can operate and evolve even when you're no longer in the room.

That is the essence of this chapter.

If the measure of a leader is what remains after they're gone, as we suggested at the very beginning of this book, then enabling capabilities is the practice that turns that philosophy into operational reality. You cannot build sustainability by remaining indispensable. You build it by making others capable of executing, solving, deciding, and creating—without you.

This is where the shift happens: from giving direction to building independence. From leading the work to leading those who will lead the work. From control to continuity.

Half of your job is delivering results today. The other half is making sure results can still be delivered once you're gone.

This chapter is about that second half.

Breaking the Development-Performance Trap

If your goal is speed, certainty, and success, you go to your best people. But if that goal includes sustainability, growth, and independence, you must balance the opposite, or risk falling into your own trap.

Organizations constantly emphasize the importance of developing their people. It appears in value statements, strategic plans, and executive speeches. Yet in daily operations, development is often the first thing to be sacrificed when results are on the line. Why? Because of a trap that most leaders fall into without realizing it: the **development-performance paradox**.

Think about how things really work in day-to-day operations. I've worked with thousands of executives across industries, and I see this pattern unfold time and again. A project lands, the deadline is tight, the client has high expectations, and the margin for error is razor thin. What does the leader do? They go straight to their most trusted person—the one who's done it before, who knows exactly how the process works, who understands the informal expectations beyond the written brief, and who will likely get it done right the first time with minimal oversight.

It's the logical move. After all, when the pressure is on, who wants to risk failure by handing off critical work to someone still learning the ropes?

So, we go to the "safe bet." The high performer. The one who has never let us down.

And then we do it again. And again. And again.

It starts innocently, as a way to protect performance. But over time, this instinct becomes a habit—and the habit becomes a system. Without meaning to, leaders start building a closed loop of dependency. Work flows to the same hands, decisions rely on the same minds, and execution depends on a shrinking circle of individuals who carry a disproportionate load. Meanwhile, everyone else remains on the sidelines, never stretched, never tested, never given a chance to prove—or improve—themselves.

This is the Development-Performance Paradox in action—where protecting performance today comes at the cost of building capability for tomorrow (See Figure V).

Development-Performance Paradox

Leaders faced with high-paced environments and short-term urgent demand for results default to focus on the proven few who can execute a task. Sacrificing development and sustainability for short term results and dependency.

**When we favor Results,
we delegate to ensure:**

- Lower Risk at Execution
- Less Time to Implement
- Less Cost Implications
- Less Investment to Coach

**But damage Development,
for fear of:**

- Higher Risk of Mistakes
- Longer Time to Implement
- Possible High-Cost Implications
- More investment in Training and Coaching

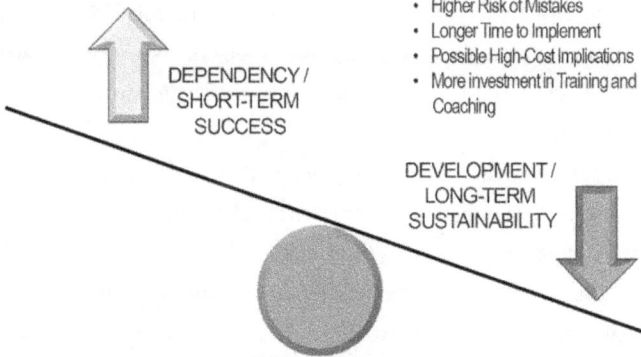

DEPENDENCY /
SHORT-TERM
SUCCESS

DEVELOPMENT /
LONG-TERM
SUSTAINABILITY

© Working Knowledge Consulting Group, 2010. © The Morphing Group, 2020

Figure V. **The Development-Performance Paradox**
This model shows the trade-off leaders make when, under pressure to deliver, they delegate to the most capable few. While this approach secures short-term results and lowers execution risk, it also increases dependency, limits development, and weakens long-term sustainability. Breaking this cycle requires shifting focus from task execution to building capability—even when the faster path seems more efficient.

This isn't just about individual leadership choices. Organizations reinforce this trap. Their systems reward those who deliver quick results, meet quarterly targets, and avoid costly mistakes. Leaders who take developmental risks—who give a project to someone new, who allow space for failure, who prioritize long-term capacity over short-term perfection—are rarely recognized. Results today are what get attention. Development, unless it's linked to a formal metric, is often invisible.

In no way am I suggesting that leaders should take every high-stakes decision and hand it over to a novice. But leadership does require discernment—and courage. Great leaders are constantly scanning for the right moments to take a development risk instead of defaulting to the comfort of quick results. This is rarely black and white. It's a scale: often gray, always contextual. But it must be navigated intentionally, not passively.

Let's Dig Our Own Grave

Some years ago, I was consulting for a big Tech company going through one of those classic turning points—when leadership finally felt pressure, not just from the market, but from the board, to get serious about succession planning. What began as a conversation about high-potential people quickly devolved into something far more revealing.

Executives started conflating performance with potential, a common but dangerous misconception. And because no one wanted to "leave anyone behind," they invented a third category: **"critical talent."** These were people they claimed the company simply *couldn't afford to lose*—not because of future leadership capacity, but because they were the only ones who knew how things worked. They held customer relationships, managed legacy systems, or carried undocumented knowledge. In short, they were irreplaceable. And, as you can imagine, it was most of the people they had nominated.

In a particularly tense meeting, I asked what I thought was an obvious question:

"Are you seriously telling me that 40% of your management team is irreplaceable?"

And then I followed with the one that no one wanted to answer: **"Do you understand the risk you've created**—not because of market volatility or regulatory pressure—but because **you've systematically chosen comfort over capability?"**

That was the moment it landed. They weren't building sustainability. They were digging their own grave—and doing it with good intentions.

The company was stable, sure. But fragile. Locked into the **development-performance paradox**—delivering results today at the cost of future resilience. They thought they were protecting value. What they were really doing was eroding it—slowly, invisibly, and entirely by design.

The uncomfortable truth is this: Many companies only confront these issues when forced to—by regulatory pressure, shareholder scrutiny, or a near-miss event. But why wait for a mandate to do what is strategically correct? Why allow yourself to build a fragile system simply because it seems to be working—for now?

Leaders who wait for a board requirement to deal with people enablement are reacting to symptoms, not addressing root causes. The point of leadership isn't to pass audits. It's to ensure the organization keeps moving, growing, and delivering—even when you or your most trusted people are no longer around.

You can choose to lead—or keep digging your company's own grave.

One of the reasons this pattern becomes so pervasive is because, quite frankly, it's easier. It is more comfortable to delegate a key task to someone who's already earned your trust than it is to invest the time in helping someone new step up. But let's be honest: That's lazy leadership. That's managing for ease, not leading for impact.

Because the job of leadership is not just to ensure execution. It is to ensure sustainability.

And the irony is this: The more you favor the few who always deliver, the more fragile your organization becomes. Because you're not the only one who isn't eternal. Your "go-to" people won't be there forever either. They'll burn out, move on, or hit their limits. And when they do, the system you built around them—rather than beyond them—won't hold.

So, while it may feel like a strategy for consistency, relying on the same few is actually a strategy for collapse.

Think about it. If we never create the space for others to try, we will never create the capacity for others to succeed. And if we don't start now, the moment we need that capacity the most, it won't be there.

In Chapter 4, we emphasized the centrality of understanding people: their aspirations, motivations, and internal drivers. One of those drivers is the need to grow. Human beings seek progress. They want to be challenged, to learn, and to know they are more capable today than they were yesterday. If leaders don't create opportunities for that to happen, they undermine one of the strongest psychological levers for engagement and performance.

Growth Requires Risk—and Leaders Must Create It

Development doesn't happen in comfort. It requires friction. It requires tension. And above all, it requires a leader who is willing to take intentional risks—not only with what they delegate, but with whom they choose to invest in.

To enable others, you must be willing to give responsibility to people who are not yet fully ready. You must accept the reality of slower results, potential mistakes, and the discomfort of watching someone else struggle through something you could've done in half the time. That is the price of growth. And it's a price most leaders claim to accept—until they feel the urgency of results knocking at the door.

It is important to keep in mind that enabling capabilities isn't about blind optimism. It's about informed bets—strategic choices where you say, "This person may not be there yet, but I believe they can be." And then, you walk beside them. You support without rescuing. You coach without taking over. You stretch without breaking. That's what it means to truly develop people.

But there's a harder reality that most leaders don't want to face. Sometimes, when you provide someone with a stretch challenge, they don't rise to it. They show you that they don't have the skills or capacity to grow beyond their current position. And that's not failure. That's information. That's leadership data. It means they deserve an honest conversation—not just about their limits, but about how they can still create value within their scope.

Even harder still, sometimes the challenge reveals that someone isn't even fit for their *current* role. And this is where many managers hide. They avoid the discomfort, pass the work to someone else, and quietly reinforce the dependency cycle—again. Instead of addressing the real issue, they sidestep it in favor of short-term execution. And in doing so, they forfeit the responsibility of leadership.

Being a leader isn't about protecting comfort. It's about protecting the organization's future. And that includes making the hard call when someone cannot meet the demands of the role—even after being given direction, support, and a real opportunity to grow. That doesn't make the person a failure. It doesn't make the leader heartless. It means you've done your part—and now, you must do the next part.

Letting go of someone who isn't the right fit is not cruelty. It's integrity. It honors the role, the team, and the person themselves. People deserve clarity. They deserve truth. They deserve a leader who won't pretend things are working when they're not.

Because varnish doesn't hold on every plank. And not every person can—or should—be carried forward. Some must be released so the team, the system, and even the individual can reset.

That, too, is leadership.

Developing the Team Without Neglecting Your Best People

Here's a leadership paradox most don't talk about: While you're try-ing to develop others, the people who are already developed—the ones you've trusted over and over again—might start to feel side-lined. They won't say it outright. But you'll notice it. The energy shifts. The engagement dips. The questions start to surface:

"Why didn't you assign that project to me?"

"Was there a reason I wasn't involved this time?"

"Is there something I need to fix?"

This isn't entitlement, it is just part of human nature. When someone has consistently been trusted with meaningful, high-impact work, their identity gets tied to that trust. Their value, in their own eyes, becomes performance-based currency: *I deliver; therefore, I matter.*

So, when you shift responsibility to someone else, it can feel to them like a withdrawal of trust. They feel unappreciated. Mistrusted. Maybe even replaced.

And that's exactly where the next leadership challenge begins.

This moment isn't just about managing egos. It's about helping your best people evolve. Because there is something important you need them to understand: Being the best individual contributor on the team is no longer the point. Their next role is not to deliver—it's to enable capabilities to deliver. It's to mentor, coach, transfer knowledge, and let go.

You're not replacing them. You're inviting them into a more strategic role: to become a multiplier, not a machine. Their value isn't diminishing—it's compounding.

And yet, many leaders get stuck here. Not just with their team, but with themselves.

Over the years, I've lost count of how many times I've been asked a version of this question:

"What do I need to learn to grow into the next role?"

And my answer is always the same:

"Start by learning how to leave your current one."

It's almost too obvious. But it's incredible how often this is over-looked. If you've made yourself indispensable, how exactly is the company supposed to let you move up? Who takes over what you've built? Who keeps the lights on when you're promoted?

Let me put it this way: If you don't have someone ready—or at least being groomed—to take on your role, then you're anchoring yourself to it. That's self-sabotage dressed as importance and disguised as loyalty.

And it extends to your team. If your best people aren't learning how to step beyond individual execution (how to provide clear direction, enable capabilities, activate performance) then they're not evolving into managers. And if some of them are already managers, but they're still stuck doing the work themselves instead of teaching others how to lead, then they're not ready for broader leadership either.

Whenever someone asks me about growing into a higher position, I flip the question:

"So, you've got someone ready to take your job today, right?"

The typical answer?

"Well, not today, no…"

And then comes the challenge:

"Then what are you doing—today—to start changing that?"

Because here's the part leaders often miss: Getting your team ready to move into your role is the clearest sign that you're ready to move into a different one. That's what leadership sustainability looks like. That's what it means to build something *without you.*

If you haven't created capacity beneath you, then you are the ceiling. And when that happens, you're not just limiting your team—you're limiting yourself.

So, while you're enabling others to grow, don't forget to enable your best people to evolve. Because when they learn to let go, to elevate others, and to multiply capacity—you finally free yourself to do the same.

Because leadership isn't about being essential. It's about building something that works—especially when you're not in the room. That's the discipline of sustainability. And enabling capabilities is how you practice it.

If no one can do your job, maybe you're not leading it. You're just holding onto it.

This is where enabling becomes real—not as a concept, but as a set of deliberate actions.

A leader who doesn't build successors is like a bridge with no other side–strong, impressive, and ultimately useless.

The idea that great leaders expand rather than centralize capability has been explored by many, perhaps most notably by Liz Wiseman in her book *Multipliers* (2010). She distinguishes between leaders who amplify the intelligence and potential of those around them ("Multipliers") and those who inadvertently diminish it by staying at the center of decisions and execution ("Diminishers").[27] While the model presented in this chapter is not based on Wiseman's framework, it shares this underlying conviction: that leadership has little to do with being a hero and a lot to do with creating more heroes. Enabling Capabilities is the discipline that makes that possible.

The following four leadership practices bring this discipline to life. Each one represents a concrete way to expand the capacity of others and to break free from the dependency loop we've just explored.

---

[27] Liz Wiseman, *Multipliers: How the Best Leaders Make Everyone Smarter* (New York: HarperBusiness, 2010).

And just like in the previous chapter, each of these practices is filtered through the fundamentals of human understanding, which present the key to better influence and lead your team into success—they are the operating system of sustainable leadership.

Practice 1: Delegate to Develop

Delegation is often misunderstood—even by experienced leaders. Most people think of it as a tactic to manage time or reduce workload. But delegation is first and foremost a leadership behavior. It's how you scale impact, develop capability, and elevate your focus.

Before you even consider *what* to delegate, the first question should be:

"What does my role actually require me to focus on?"

Not *"What am I good at?"*

Not *"What can I do faster or better than my team?"*

This is one of the most common traps for newly promoted leaders—especially those who've been recognized for strong execution. They move into a bigger role but continue doing the work of their old one. Not because they're bad leaders, but because they haven't yet redefined their value.

Leadership is not about proving your competence. It's about creating conditions where others can deliver. Delegation is how you start letting go of what you used to prove yourself with and step into the work that only you can now do: setting direction, aligning effort, enabling growth, and activating performance.

And this becomes even more critical in situations where companies finally do what they should've done all along: promote someone not because of their technical expertise, but because of their leadership capacity. I've seen it happen—an operations leader put in charge of HR. Or a finance leader given the reins of a product team. People often question those moves. *"How can they lead a function they've*

127

never worked in?" But here's the thing: They're not there to be the expert. They're there to lead the experts.

They were chosen not because they know the tools—but because they understand the system. They know the business model, the strategy, and the leadership practices that make organizations effective. And if that's true, then their success won't come from their individual brilliance or knowledge—it will come from how well they delegate, empower, and develop the people around them.

Questions Leaders Should Ask Themselves:

- What are the strategic expectations of my role that only I can deliver?
- Am I delegating to grow someone, or just to get something off my plate?
- Who on my team hasn't had a meaningful challenge in a while?
- Am I avoiding delegating to someone because I doubt their capacity? And if so, what am I going to do about it—instead of continuing to avoid it?
- Who could surprise me if I gave them a real opportunity?

Why This Practice Matters Through the Lens of Human Understanding

At its core, delegation is about trust—and trust is one of the most powerful psychological signals a leader can send. When you delegate something meaningful, you're not just giving someone a task—you're telling them: *"I see potential in you."* That message—if delivered well—can activate deep motivation. It makes people want to rise to the occasion, not because they're told to, but because they've been invited to grow.

From a human processing standpoint, delegation affects multiple layers of behavior:

- **Delegation clarifies roles, expectations, and the broader scope of leadership work**. It helps people see how things connect beyond their current responsibilities. But for delegation to truly become developmental, you have to go further. You must address not only your expectations, but also the challenges you foresee. That requires knowing your people—their strengths and weaknesses—and being forthcoming. Let them know where you see risk, and let them know who they can rely on (whether it's you or someone else). That's not control. That's preparation.

- **When delegation is framed as a stretch—not a setup—people are far more likely to embrace it, even if it makes them uncomfortable.** They feel chosen, not dumped on. And that matters especially when the task is something unexpected or outside their perceived readiness. Remember, development requires discomfort. You need to help them see **why** this stretch will be meaningful and how it will serve them in the future.

- **Ownership triggers initiative**. When someone truly feels that something is theirs to lead, performance shifts from compliance to commitment. But there's a critical condition: delegation requires authority. There's nothing more frustrating than being handed responsibility with no power to make decisions. Even if your team doesn't ask for it, it's your job as the leader to clarify authority boundaries. Make it clear what they own, where they can decide, and what falls outside their lane.

- **Repeated, thoughtful delegation builds psychological safety and team resilience**. Over time, people learn that their development matters more to you than their immediate perfection. And when you delegate to one person in order to develop them, don't pretend otherwise. Be candid. Say it out loud: *"I'm giving this to your teammate so they can grow. We need more people who can lead in this space."*

That transparency builds trust—both with the person you're delegating to and with the rest of the team.

And don't forget: Involving your high-potential talent in coaching and mentoring their peers is also a powerful development opportunity for them. They, too, must learn to move beyond being indispensable executors—and start becoming leaders who build the success of others.

- **Every time a delegated task is followed by coaching, reflection, and feedback**—not just evaluation—it reinforces both the behavior and the belief: *"I can grow into more."* People are not plug-and-play. Not even your high-potentials. In fact, the more ambitious or creative someone is, the more support, feedback, and adjustment they'll need. That's not weakness—that's signal. Use it.

And here's something critical: Once you delegate, you have to stay the course. Few things erode trust more than a leader who changes direction mid-way because they've decided they could do it better.

Even worse is delegating a task while quietly lining up someone else to prepare a backup "just in case." That's not risk management—it's sabotage. It signals you don't actually believe in the person you chose, and it fractures accountability across the team. Delegation requires commitment. If you need to change course, be transparent and own the impact—on both the outcome and the relationship.

Leaders earn trust not by controlling everything, but by standing behind the decisions they make about others.

Because when delegation is missing—or misused—people draw fast conclusions. They start to believe that only a few are trusted with real responsibility. That their job is to execute, not grow. That performance matters more than potential.

Delegation isn't just about getting work done. **It's a message. And people hear that message—clearly.**

Practice 2: Accompany with Intent

Accompaniment is one of the most misunderstood leadership practices, because it lives in the gray area between micromanaging and abandoning. It's not about hovering. And it's not about disappearing either. It's about showing up with purpose and staying with someone through the discomfort of learning and growth.

To accompany someone with intent means staying close enough to support their progress without removing their ownership. It's being present not just physically, but mentally—observing, asking, coaching, and stepping in only when the moment calls for it. But more than that, it means understanding how *who they are*—not just *what they know*—will shape how they approach the challenge.

People don't enter development spaces blank. They bring their history with them. They lean on their dominant traits—the behaviors that got them results in the past. Sometimes that works. But sometimes, what made someone successful before is exactly what will get in the way now.

A leader's job is to see that coming.

If you know someone tends to be highly autocratic and you place them in a cross-functional team that thrives on collaboration, you're not just delegating a task—you're handing them a leadership mirror. And your role doesn't end with assigning the challenge. You have to stay present, not as a passive observer, but as an active guide. Help them see where their default behaviors may cause tension. Help them experiment with new approaches. Help them realize that strengths overused can become derailers.

Accompaniment isn't a neutral act. It's a leadership choice. It means you're not just watching someone struggle—you're working to make sure they succeed. And that includes the hardest part: helping them see that growth sometimes means letting go of what used to work.

Questions Leaders Should Ask Themselves:

- Do I stay close enough to support—or too close to control?
- When someone is struggling, do I step in too soon—or disappear too fast?
- Am I present during the learning curve, or only visible at the start and the end?
- Have I helped this person see how their usual approach might be limiting them here?
- Do I create time to reflect with people—or just monitor their progress?

Why This Practice Matters Through the Lens of Human Understanding

Growth almost always comes with resistance. Even when people want to learn, learning threatens identity. It introduces uncertainty, exposes gaps, and temporarily shakes confidence. That's human nature.

And this is exactly when many leaders vanish. They believe they're empowering someone by "getting out of the way," but in reality, they've withdrawn support at the moment it's most needed. As the person steps into new challenges, their natural discomfort is seen by the leader as a lack of readiness. The normal learning curve is misread as evidence of failure.

This is where accompaniment matters most.

- **People are far more likely to lean into discomfort when they feel seen—not judged.** When a leader stays close without suffocating, it creates the emotional space needed to accept the challenge for what it is: growth, not threat. And when the challenge includes unlearning what's made them successful, your presence becomes even more essential.
- Leaders often say, "I trust you," but then disappear until review time. **Real trust is shown through presence**—by observing, listening, and signaling that you're still invested in the outcome, even if you're not driving it. Especially when someone is

wrestling with the friction between who they've been and who they need to become, your trust becomes a stabilizer.

- **When leaders are present** during the messy middle—not just for the outcome—**they create moments for reflection, feedback, and encouragement.** This is where self-belief is built. This is where new behaviors are tested. And this is where people begin to internalize their own capability—not just to succeed, but to evolve.

Accompaniment doesn't mean handholding. It means staying with the learner long enough for them to find their footing—even when that means helping them recognize that the old playbook doesn't apply anymore.

Let's address a comment I often hear when working with leaders: **"When will I do my job if I have to babysit everyone?"**

Here's the hard truth: If you see this kind of leadership as babysitting, you haven't yet understood what the role truly demands. As we've already stated, *this is your job*. This is what leadership means. You're not just driving outcomes—you're building the capability that will remain once you're gone. And yes, that takes time. But the more you practice this, the more precise and surgical you'll become. Presence doesn't mean hovering over everything—it means being intentional about where and how you show up.

Second, this is exactly why leaders need to ask themselves what they should really be focusing on. Most are buried in endless, low-value meetings that create the illusion of productivity—what W.J. Reddin famously called *"apparent effectiveness."*[28] Just because you're busy doesn't mean you're doing meaningful work. And that's the real trap. We say we don't have time to develop people, but we always seem to have time for rework, escalations, and crisis management—the very symptoms of not developing people in the first place.

If you don't make time for accompaniment, your calendar will make time for the consequences.

---

[28] W. J. Reddin, *Managerial Effectiveness* (New York: McGraw-Hill, 1970).

Practice 3: Feedback That Moves People

Feedback is one of the most powerful—and most misused—tools a leader has. Most leaders think they're giving it. Most team members think they're not receiving it. And in many cases, both are technically right.

That's because most feedback is vague, one-sided, or delivered at the wrong time for the wrong reasons. Leaders give it when something goes wrong, or when they've already made a judgment. And employees brace for it as if it were punishment. But effective feedback—the kind that enables learning and change—isn't about judgment. It's about development. It's not about telling someone how they did. It's about helping them understand what they can do next—and how.

Giving feedback that enables means providing insight that is timely, specific, and framed in a way that moves the person forward. It's about shining a light on patterns, not isolated incidents. It's about tying feedback to the person's potential—not just their performance. And most of all, it's about creating the conditions for change: understanding, acceptance, and action.

Over the last 15 years, I've gathered data across industries, regions, and company sizes—thousands of data points—studying how leaders apply the practices we're discussing in this book. And one pattern has remained painfully consistent: **Feedback is the lowest-rated practice, year after year.**

This isn't a perception issue. It's a performance one. Across contexts, leaders struggle to provide feedback that actually enables growth.

And it's not hard to see why. Unlike other leadership practices, feedback is deeply personal and highly variable. What works with one person can backfire with another. You may craft the perfect message—clear, timely, constructive—and still be met with resistance, defensiveness, or silence. Because feedback doesn't exist in a vacuum. It lands in someone's psychology, in their story, in their fears and assumptions. That means your approach has to change with each person if you want it to be effective—and the only way to develop that judgment is through experience, reflection, and practice.

That's what makes feedback hard. It's also what makes it essential.

If feedback doesn't produce movement—if the person doesn't shift how they see, think, or act—then it failed. Not necessarily because it was wrong, but most likely because it didn't reach them.

Instead of focusing on delivering your message, focus on achieving the outcome. Too many leaders leave a feedback conversation thinking, *"There, I said it."* when what really matters is, *"Did they get it?"* Feedback isn't about saying what you needed to say. It's about helping the other person hear it, believe it, and grow from it.

When you ask that, everything changes. You stop focusing on your delivery and start thinking about what will actually create change for the person in front of you. That shift is what transforms feedback from a risky moment into a leadership lever.

One thing I've seen repeatedly—anecdotally but consistently—is that the higher someone rises in leadership, the less feedback they give. It's understandable: They're pulled into strategy, further from day-to-day execution, and often forget how powerful their words can be. But feedback is much more than an execution tool, it should always be used as a development lever.

And development doesn't stop with seniority. If feedback is going to take root in an organization, it has to start at the top. Still, if your boss doesn't model it, that's no excuse. You decide what type of leader you want to be, regardless of the type of leader you have. Start with your team.

Because feedback shouldn't be just a conversation. It's primarily a leadership responsibility.

And most companies are still getting it wrong—until someone decides to lead differently.

Questions Leaders Should Ask Themselves:

- Do I give feedback regularly—or only when something goes wrong or during annual reviews?
- When I give feedback, is it framed for learning or evaluation? Do I prepare with intent?
- Am I addressing observable, repeated behavior-outcome patterns—or making it personal?
- Do I deliver feedback in a way the other person can understand and act on?
- Have I created a trusting environment where people feel safe to receive feedback—and to give it back?

Why This Practice Matters Through the Lens of Human Understanding

Feedback is rarely received in the spirit it was intended. That's because feedback isn't processed logically—it's filtered through emotion, identity, and psychological safety. For many, even well-meaning feedback triggers defensiveness, shame, or fear of failure. That's why how you give feedback matters as much as what you say.

- **People can't improve if they don't understand what needs to change**. Effective feedback gives clarity—not just on what happened, but on why it matters and what to do next. Remember people react better if they believe acting on the feedback you provide will matter to them.
- **People need to feel that feedback is rooted in development, not judgment**. When feedback is framed as an investment in their growth—and delivered with respect—they're far more likely to listen without shutting down.
- **Feedback only works if it's actionable—and personal**. Vague advice like *"I need you to be more strategic"* doesn't help, unless you clarify what you mean by that. But even clear feedback can fall flat if it doesn't land with the person you're speaking to.

People filter feedback through identity, emotion, and past experience. That means your delivery must be just as thoughtful as your message.

- **Feedback lands best when there's a foundation of trust—not just in your intentions, but in your judgment.** If the person doesn't believe you have their growth in mind or doesn't think you've earned the credibility to assess their performance, they'll tune out—even if you're right. Vulnerability matters here too. If you've failed to give clear direction or support in the past, acknowledge it. Feedback works best when people sense it's coming from someone who's invested, competent, and fair.

- **Follow up. Feedback that disappears after the conversation is just noise**. But when you circle back, acknowledge progress, and show that you noticed the effort, it reinforces not just the behavior—but the belief that change is possible.

People crave feedback—not the kind that knocks them down, but the kind that helps them level up. They want to know someone sees their potential and is willing to help them get there.

And one last thing—feedback, when done right, is selfless. It only works when you genuinely have the other person's best interest in mind. If your goal is just to unload everything sitting on your chest, go ahead—see how that goes. But if your goal is to improve your team's performance (which, by the way, is in your own best interest too), then it starts with this: Make sure every person on your team gets a fair share of your time and attention to help them grow. That's how you build something that outlasts you—by investing your time, your preparation, and your interest in the people you lead.

Practice 4: Empower with Boundaries

Empowerment is a word that gets thrown around a lot—often with good intentions, but vague execution. Leaders say they want people to take initiative, make decisions, and own their work. But when there's no clarity on the limits, no structure around authority, and no alignment on expectations, empowerment turns into chaos—or worse, a setup for failure.

Many organizations still operate in deeply hierarchical ways—where authority is tiered, decisions funnel upward, and empowerment is more rhetoric than reality. Over time, this breeds not just frustration, but comfort. Teams get used to not deciding. Why take a risk when your boss will eventually own the outcome? The longer this dynamic persists, the more initiative erodes—and with it, accountability and speed. Empowerment starts dying long before anyone realizes it.

To truly empower someone, you need to do two things at once: **Give them space** and **define the space.** That means being explicit about where they can act freely, where they should consult, and where they must not cross. It means defining the "why," the "what," and the "where"—but letting them own the "how."

Empowering with boundaries isn't about control. It's about **creating the conditions where autonomy thrives without jeopardizing alignment.** And it's one of the most overlooked disciplines in leadership today.

And here's the hard part: Empowerment can feel like loss. Many leaders resist letting go of decisions not because they don't believe in their people—but because it challenges their own value. *If I'm no longer needed for the tough calls, what's my role?* But that's the trap. You are doing your best leadership work when your team no longer depends on you. Leaders fear irrelevance, but it's the very path to building a legacy.

Questions Leaders Should Ask Themselves:

- Have I made it clear what decisions someone can make without me?
- Do I explain what outcomes I expect, or do I only delegate tasks?
- When someone hesitates, is it due to lack of capability—or lack of clarity?
- Do people know where the boundaries are—or are they just guessing?
- Am I willing to let people work differently, as long as they deliver?

Why This Practice Matters Through the Lens of Human Understanding

People want autonomy—but only when it feels safe. And safety comes from knowing where the guardrails are. When people don't know what's expected, they hold back. When they fear overstepping, they default to inaction. When they're empowered without clarity, they don't feel free—they feel set up.

- **Empowerment begins with clarity**. If people don't understand what they own, they won't act. Leaders must define roles, expectations, and decision rights clearly—and revisit them often. And let's be clear: Empowerment doesn't just fail because of leadership behaviors—it often fails because of system design. The operating model and organizational architecture can either reinforce autonomy or suffocate it. I've seen leaders tasked with chasing million-dollar deals who can't approve a $200 expense. What message does that send? Empowerment only works when authority is backed by systems that trust people to act.
- **People are more likely to take ownership when they know the leader still cares about outcomes**. Boundaries signal structure—not micromanagement. When the framework is clear, initiative feels like a responsibility, not a risk.

139

- **True empowerment gives permission to move**. But without clear zones of authority, people stall, or overreach. If you want people to act, make it unmistakable where they can. Many companies talk obsessively about innovation yet actively disempower their people. They host ideation workshops, promote "creative sprints," and invite new ideas, but still require approvals for every decision, punish initiative when it backfires, and restrict the very space needed for experimentation.

  But real innovation requires real empowerment. People need to feel they can challenge norms, suggest what hasn't been tried, and decide to act on new ideas. If the message is, "Innovate, but don't move," you won't get innovation. You'll get compliance wrapped in creative theater.

- **When people operate within clear boundaries and succeed, trust builds**. Not just between leader and team, but within the team itself. People stop second-guessing and start collaborating. But trust goes beyond permissions. Mixed signals kill empowerment. A team leader can't preach autonomy and then block people from sharing information across teams without approval. You can't tell people they're empowered and then treat them like liabilities. Empowerment starts with trust—not blind, but guided, built through decision-making, follow-up, and reflection.

- **When empowered work leads to results, acknowledge it.** Highlight not just the outcome, but the ownership. That tells the team: *This is what we want more of.*

People don't need endless freedom. They need clear space to lead—without tripping over hidden wires.

One final trap to watch for: Many leaders confuse empowerment with absence. They believe that empowering someone means stepping away completely. Then, when a mistake inevitably happens, they pull the responsibility back—telling themselves, *"See? This is why I have to stay involved."* And just like that, the cycle restarts.

This is a key takeaway: Empowerment isn't a switch—it's a process. And it's especially difficult in organizations that aren't used to it. It's not just the leaders who need to change; it's the entire system. People who have spent years without decision rights don't suddenly embrace accountability the moment you hand it over. It's uncomfortable. It's unfamiliar. It takes time.

That's why building a culture of empowerment requires more than delegation—it requires intention, and organizational support. The systems, processes and policies of a company must endorse it and embrace it.

Leaders and companies must prepare for it. They need a structured plan. Coaching at every level. Leaders need to trust before trust is fully earned. Teams need to stretch before they're fully ready. You don't wait for people to be "empowerable." You empower, and then you develop. Otherwise, all you're doing is rehearsing the same frustration—again and again.

Leadership is not a spotlight—it's a scaffold. Your role is not to shine at the center, but to build the structure that lets others rise, stretch, and eventually stand on their own. If you're still the hero, you haven't yet built the stage.

Looking Ahead: From Capability to Commitment

Enabling Capabilities is one of the most tangible ways leaders build legacy. It is the work of creating capability, independence, and momentum in others. It's what separates leaders who hold things together from those who build something that lasts. When you enable, you stop being the pillar everyone leans on and become the architect of something that stands without you. That's the foundation of sustainable leadership. That's what it means to build without you.

In this chapter, we've explored the four essential practices that turn intent into capability:

- **Delegate to Develop**—assigning with purpose to create growth, not just get things done.
- **Accompany with Intent**—being present to coach, support, and stretch without rescuing.
- **Give Feedback that Moves People**—using insight to generate real change, not just commentary.
- **Empower with Boundaries**—building autonomy with structure so initiative becomes safe and sustainable.

What follows is not easier leadership. It is more meaningful leadership. The kind that gets results today while preparing others to carry those results into tomorrow.

In the next chapter, we will shift from empowering action to **activating value creation**—the motivational core of leadership that turns performance into purpose and effort into meaning. It is where execution meets belief and where sustainable results become personal.

Chapter 7: The Practices of Activating Value Creation

Before diving into the critical practices of activating value creation, I'd like to take a moment to focus on two key parts of that phrase. Let's start with the latter: **value creation**. It's a term we use often but rarely stop to define. What does it actually mean to create value?

The answer is not singular. Value can be created in different ways, for different stakeholders, and with different consequences. For some, it might mean profitability. For others, innovation. For a team member, it may mean meaningful work or professional growth. For society, it could be ethical impact or long-term improvement of the surroundings. The value that's created depends not only on what is produced, but on who receives it, how it's delivered, and whether it endures.

Several established perspectives help frame this more clearly.

Michael Porter's *Value Chain* model emphasizes the activities within an organization that, when optimized, lead to competitive advantage.[29] Meanwhile, the *Service-Dominant Logic* proposed by Vargo and Lusch reframes value not as something embedded in a product,

---

[29] Michael E. Porter, *Competitive Advantage: Creating and Sustaining Superior Performance* (New York: Free Press, 1985), 33–61.

but as something co-created through interaction and use.[30] Stakeholder Theory expands the lens even further—asserting that real value is created when organizations serve the needs of all stakeholders, not just shareholders.[31]

What these perspectives share is this: **Value is not static, and it is not created in isolation**. It's dynamic, context-dependent, and most importantly, it is **co-created**.

Now, if we follow the belief that it is the leader alone who must create that value, we fall into a familiar trap: the myth of the self-sufficient leader. The one who gets things done. The all-knowing problem solver. The organizational savior. But that is not really leadership, and focusing on playing that role is what gets many leaders to limit their own ceiling.

Leadership should not be focused on creating all the value yourself. It's about **activating value creation**—building the infrastructure, culture, and conditions so that together with others you can create, contribute, and deliver value in ways that extend beyond the leader's reach.

And that brings us to the first word in the phrase: **activation**.

To activate is not to direct, control, or extract. It is to spark, enable, and expand. Activation means moving yourself and others into a position where value creation becomes possible—deliberate, collective, and sustainable.

And that is a fundamentally different approach to leadership.

True Sustainable Leadership isn't about creating value—it's about activating others to create it.

---

[30] Stephen L. Vargo and Robert F. Lusch, "Evolving to a New Dominant Logic for Marketing," *Journal of Marketing* 68, no. 1 (January 2004): 1–17, https://doi.org/10.1509/jmkg.68.1.1.24036.
[31] R. Edward Freeman, *Strategic Management: A Stakeholder Approach* (Boston: Pitman, 1984).

Value Creation Requires More Than Execution

Many leaders assume their role is to drive task completion, meet deadlines, and achieve short-term goals. And while those things matter, they are not the full extent of a leader's responsibility. A leader's true role is to create the conditions where value can be continuously created—not just produced by force or repetition, but activated by people's insight, energy, and initiative.

That value doesn't come from doing more of the same. It comes from detecting opportunities, solving problems differently, and connecting people's efforts to something bigger. In other words, value creation today depends on **the collective intelligence and contribution of others**, not just on the leader's ability to decide and direct.

Efficiency has limits. It creates economic value through speed and cost control, but it rarely leads to transformation. Leaders who want to create value must look beyond efficiency and begin activating value creation across their teams—that is, unlocking the willingness, creativity, and ownership of the people they lead.

And here's the challenge:

You can't activate others unless they feel they are part of what's being built.

The Missed Opportunity: What Frontline Voices Reveal About Value Creation

I've had the opportunity to work with several companies that embarked on bottom-up initiatives—whether to rethink their purpose, innovate around product offerings, improve customer experience, or eliminate inefficiencies. Instead of highlighting one story, I'll share a common pattern I've seen play out across different industries and geographies.

When leaders open themselves to listening—and I mean truly listening—to the people on the frontline, those who operate the machinery, who use the systems, who face the customer, or who serve

145

as the buffer between expectation and delivery, they discover something eye-opening: Many things are not working as they think they are.

I've seen leaders convinced that all is running smoothly, only to later realize their teams are navigating a tangle of unnecessary steps, outdated procedures, bureaucratic dead ends, client-frustrating workarounds, and process layers that delay, rigidize, and dull the overall experience of working with (or inside) the company.

And here's the part that repeats itself almost everywhere I go: The frontline frequently has a good idea of what is not working. They usually have several thoughts on how to improve it. And they don't act—because they believe they're not allowed to.

That's the tragedy. I've seen companies cut delivery times, reduce costs, and even reshape entire service models—not through high-level strategic redesign, but by finally listening to people who had been quietly carrying the burden and waiting for permission to fix it.

And I've also seen the opposite: Internal idea contests launched for show, with no commitment to act. Recognition programs that fostered competition, not culture. Teams that gained momentum and trust, only to be broken apart by leaders who feared being overshadowed.

Here's the bottom line: Value creation requires courage.

It demands that leaders believe in something many are not taught to trust: that the collective intelligence, perspective, and capacity of the people around them will often surpass, by far, their own ability to create the new and different.

And that scares some people in leadership positions. It makes them feel replaceable. It shakes their identity and disrupts their sense of control.

But in truth, their value increases when they build the environment where others can thrive—especially when they are no longer in the room. It takes courage to lead so well you're no longer needed.

146

If You Don't Feel Included, Why Would You Contribute?

Let's set the record straight: Whatever connotations the term may have acquired in recent times, **inclusion is not a political concept**. It has played a key role since the dawn of humanity and is deeply tied to our gregarious instincts. It's more than meeting quotas or simulating interest in other people's opinions. It's about being genuinely open to the idea that everyone has something to contribute—and that there is real value in considering different ways of thinking.

Inclusion is a leadership discipline. It's about creating conditions where people's presence matters, their ideas influence outcomes, and their contribution is seen as valuable.

People seldom innovate in places where they feel ignored. They rarely suggest improvements in cultures where they are barely heard. And they are certainly less likely to go the extra mile in environments where they are treated as interchangeable parts.

Inclusion is the missing link between motivation and ownership. You can give direction and enable capability, but if someone doesn't feel connected—if they aren't seen or valued—they will not contribute their full potential.

And I know—for many in leadership positions, that's just... acceptable. Some genuinely believe there's little to gain from listening to people in the lower ranks of the organization. After all, what could they possibly add to the complexities of the business?

Yes, a company can survive by simply having people execute the tasks assigned to them. In fact, most companies operate this way. But I've seen firsthand the true competitive advantage that only a few achieve—the ones that challenge this ancient belief. When tribes are formed, when connections run deep, when people give more **not because they were asked to, but because they were noticed**— that's when something extraordinary happens.

If you want value, you have to unlock it. And that means making space for people to care, to challenge, to propose, and to create. Inclusion is how you do that.

And inclusion isn't only about who gets to speak or contribute—it's also about who gets to be part of the story. When a leader shares a story that highlights someone's effort, learning, or impact, they are not just transferring knowledge—they are weaving that person into the cultural fabric of the team. Storytelling, when used with intention, is a powerful act of inclusion. It tells people: "You matter here. What you did shaped who we are becoming."

The same goes for recognition. Honoring someone's contribution is not about ceremony—it's about acknowledgment. When people are seen, when their work is named, when their role in success is made visible, they feel a deeper sense of belonging. They don't just feel appreciated—they feel included.

> *If you don't see the person, don't expect the performance.*

The Value Activation Framework™

Five Conditions That Unlock Human Contribution

As we've said before, organizations don't unlock value simply by asking for more output—they do it by creating the right conditions for people to contribute with intent, energy, and insight. That kind of contribution is not automatic. It requires a leadership approach that goes beyond directing tasks and begins enabling others to bring their best forward.

Just as Chapter 5 introduced the 7 Factors of Organizational Effectiveness™ to structure alignment, and Chapter 6 used the Development-Performance Paradox to understand how people grow, this chapter introduces an additional model—one that helps activate value through human contribution at all levels.

We call this model the **Value Activation Framework™**. It outlines five core conditions that unlock contribution—not just from leaders, but across the organization. These are not one-off initiatives. They are **shared dynamics** that need to be cultivated by everyone: leaders, peers, teams, and individuals alike. Everyone has a role to play in creating an environment where ideas flow, stories are shared, contributions are acknowledged, and people feel they belong.

Value Activation Framework™

© Working Knowledge Consulting Group, 2010. © The Morphing Group, 2020

*Figure VI. **The Value Activation Framework™***
This model illustrates the five key behaviors that activate value creation within teams and organizations: inviting thinking, acknowledging identity, sharing the why and the how, celebrating meaningfully, and building confidence and safety. Everyone on the team plays a role in bringing these behaviors to life through daily actions. Leaders, however, have the critical responsibility of cultivating the environment where these practices can thrive—modeling, reinforcing, and amplifying the behaviors that drive sustainable engagement, inclusion, and innovation.

While leaders must take the initiative to shape these conditions, activating value is not the result of isolated leadership actions. It is the product of **organizational dynamics**—living systems built through the continuous interactions, recognitions, and contributions of everyone involved. True value creation becomes sustainable only when it moves beyond intention and becomes embedded in how people think, relate, and work together every day.

1. **Invite Thinking** - *People must feel their ideas are welcomed.* Value creation doesn't happen in echo chambers. When people believe their thinking is respected—especially when it challenges the norm—they stay curious, speak up, and contribute more. But this openness must be modeled across the organization. Everyone shares responsibility for asking, listening, and making space for different perspectives. Leaders set the tone, but teams bring it to life.

2. **Acknowledge Identity** - *People must feel seen for who they are.* True inclusion goes beyond roles—it recognizes the person behind the work. When people's values, stories, and motivations are acknowledged, they show up with more energy and commitment. Every member of a team plays a role in this—through empathy, respect, and recognition of each other's context. For leaders, it means actively honoring individual differences instead of expecting uniformity.

3. **Share the Why and the How** - *People must see how they fit into something larger.*
    Stories are how people find meaning. When the narrative of progress includes individual and team contributions—not just abstract goals—people feel they belong to the journey. Culture is shaped by the stories we tell and who we include in them. Everyone contributes to that narrative through how they speak about success and acknowledge others. Leaders, however, carry special weight in reinforcing shared meaning.

4. **Celebrate Meaningfully** - *People must know their efforts matter.* Celebration isn't about parties or rewards—it's about honoring contribution. When people feel their efforts are noticed and appreciated, they're more likely to engage and reinvest. Recognition should be cultural, not positional. Peers can celebrate each

other. Teams can honor growth. But leaders must make celebration intentional, public, and tied to values—not just outcomes.

5. **Build Confidence and Safety -** *People must feel they can take risks.* Nothing shuts down contribution like fear. When people believe they'll be punished for disagreeing, experimenting, or failing, they withdraw. Psychological safety must be collective: Teammates protect each other, not just themselves. But leaders shape this condition most directly—through how they respond to dissent, how they handle mistakes, and whether they treat risk-taking as a sign of strength.

Activating value is not the responsibility of leaders alone—it lives in the day-to-day interactions, acknowledgments, and contributions of everyone in the organization. These dynamics take root when people consistently reinforce them through how they think, work, and relate. But for them to endure, leadership must intentionally model and amplify them, and the organization itself must align its systems, structures, and rewards to support the culture it seeks to build. Without reinforcement from leadership and organizational design, even the best intentions eventually erode.

In the following section, we will explore what leaders can do—specifically and intentionally—to activate these conditions and make them part of everyday practice. These practices are not just cultural ideals. They are leadership disciplines that directly activate value creation—by making people understand they belong, their ideas count, their impact is real, and their story is part of something bigger.

Practice 1: Understand and Embrace What Moves Others

People don't create value when they are simply completing tasks—they create it when their efforts are fueled by something that resonates personally. Value creation begins when individuals contribute not just their skills, but their energy, ideas, and ownership.

151

And that kind of contribution is only unlocked when the work connects to what matters to them.

We briefly explored this in Chapter 4, where we discussed how motivation is shaped by individual drivers and internal narratives. But here, we take it further. In this practice, the goal is not just to understand what moves others—it's to **accept and embrace** that what motivates them may be fundamentally different from what motivates you. That difference isn't a complication—it's a resource. Leaders who assume their team shares the same values and aspirations are likely to misread behavior, miss opportunities, and underutilize potential.

Inclusion, in this context, means recognizing and respecting the diversity of motivators in your team. It's the willingness to see different definitions of meaning as legitimate—even when they don't align with your own. It's about making room for people to care about different things and adjusting your leadership accordingly.

When leaders do this—when they create space for people to connect their own sense of purpose to their role—what emerges is not just engagement, but energy. People begin to contribute with intention, not just obligation. And that's where value is created—not from uniformity, but from personal investment brought into a shared direction.

Questions Leaders Should Ask Themselves:

- Do I understand—and accept—what truly drives each person on my team, even when it's different from what drives me?
- Do I ever assume that my motivators are "better," "stronger," or "more serious" than theirs?
- Have I created space where people feel safe expressing what they want—not just what they're expected to do?
- Do I get curious when someone's energy dips—or do I judge it?

Why This Practice Matters Through the Lens of Human Understanding

- **People respond to what they perceive—and they seek validation in what matters to them.** When a leader dismisses or overlooks someone's internal drivers, the person doesn't just feel unseen—they feel undervalued. When those motivators are respected and reinforced, people are more likely to invest, commit, and create.

- **Motivation is not static—it shifts with time, experience, and context.** Leaders who assume they "already know" what drives someone often miss the moment when things change. Staying attuned to people's evolving drivers is essential for keeping them engaged and committed.

- **People only open up about what they truly want when they feel safe to do so.** Without trust and psychological safety, most people will stick to surface-level responses. If leaders want to understand what moves others, they need to create the conditions for honesty and self-expression.

- **People invest more when their work connects to what they care about.** When there's alignment between personal meaning and the role they play, people bring more initiative, creativity, and resilience. Value creation becomes more sustainable because it's fueled from within, not imposed from above.

You can't activate what you don't understand. People don't create value just because they're told to—they do it when what they do connects to who they are. That means curiosity must become a leadership discipline, not an occasional gesture. When someone feels seen, their energy changes. Their commitment shifts.

And when that happens, you're no longer managing effort—you're unleashing it.

Practice 2: Make Room for Other Ways of Thinking

Most of the value that gets created in organizations doesn't come from repeating what already works—it comes from challenging it. New ideas, different approaches, and unexpected insights are the real drivers of innovation and improvement.

But none of that is possible if people feel that only one way of thinking is accepted: the leader's way.

Leaders often get to their roles by having the answers. But if they hold too tightly to that mindset, they become the biggest barrier to progress. Making room for other ways of thinking isn't about being nice or weak—it's about ensuring that your team can see and solve more than you ever could on your own.

And when people don't feel safe to offer a different view, the risk isn't just silence—it's false agreement. This is where leaders fall into the "emperor has no clothes" trap: They interpret quiet nods or polite affirmations as genuine buy-in, unaware that dissent has gone underground. Later, they're surprised when execution stalls, resistance surfaces, or outcomes fall short—not realizing that the people involved never truly believed in the plan to begin with.

Inclusion here means creating psychological space for challenge, exploration, and dissent. It means treating different perspectives not as noise, but as the raw material of innovation. It requires humility to accept that your view is limited, and courage to invite others to expand it—even if that means hearing what you don't want to hear.

Questions Leaders Should Ask Themselves:

- Do I create the kind of environment where disagreement is encouraged—or quietly penalized?
- When someone challenges my ideas, do I see it as a threat to control—or as a sign of strength in the team?
- Have I made it clear, both through words and behavior, that people are safe to express a different point of view?

- Do I tend to default to familiar voices and thinking patterns, or do I actively bring in new perspectives?
- Am I more invested in being right—or in seeing the best ideas win, regardless of where they come from?
- And beyond my own behavior—am I encouraging my team to lead this way with their people?

Why This Practice Matters Through the Lens of Human Understanding

- **People interpret leadership through consistency of behavior.** If you ask for input but dismiss it—or defend your position every time—people quickly learn that the invitation isn't real. Over time, they disengage, and the best thinking never surfaces.
- **Psychological safety is a precondition for contribution.** People don't challenge, propose, or innovate in environments where the cost of dissent feels higher than the benefit of honesty.
- **Without inclusion, teams default to passive agreement.** When people sense their thinking won't matter, they stay silent—or worse, nod in agreement and later resist passively. This is how false alignment erodes execution from the inside out.
- **Cognitive diversity only creates value when it's activated.** Bringing together different profiles and perspectives is not enough. If those voices don't influence direction, the system becomes performative rather than productive.

Contribution doesn't happen in silence. When people hold back their perspective, they're also holding back their value—and usually for a reason. Whether it's fear of judgment, habit, or hierarchy, silence is rarely neutral. That's why your role as a leader isn't just to allow dissent—it's to actively invite it, reward it, and model how to navigate it. Ask for the counterpoint. Thank the challenge. Let others see how constructive friction drives better thinking.

155

The moment people realize their ideas won't be dismissed instantly—or used against them—is the moment they start showing up differently. They speak with more confidence, challenge more openly, and take more responsibility for what's being created.

Many leaders avoid opening discussions on new ideas when they believe they already have the answer. This is exactly where the Development–Results Paradox comes into play. Instead of recognizing the value of a rich exchange that could lead to insight or innovation, they shut it down in the name of "efficient decision-making." But what they're really doing is limiting development, weakening engagement, and closing the door on potential breakthroughs. Because when disagreement is met with curiosity instead of control, you unlock more than ideas—you unlock commitment. That's when people stop merely participating and start taking ownership.

Practice 3: Make It Theirs—Share the Why and the How

People don't create value when they are told what to do. They create value when they understand why it matters—and feel they have a say in how it's done.

When leaders withhold context or control process, they rob people of the meaning and ownership that spark real contribution. But when leaders share the story—why we're doing this, how it connects to something bigger, and where the team can shape it—they open a door to agency, insight, and alignment.

This isn't about delivering charismatic speeches. It's about connecting the dots between strategy and personal meaning. Storytelling becomes a leadership function—not for inspiration alone, but to make the journey feel real. It creates a throughline from intention to action. And inclusion, here, means bringing people into the story— not as passive listeners, but as co-authors of how that story unfolds.

And while this book won't go deep into storytelling methods— there are already excellent resources for that (and we encourage you to explore them)—what matters most is this: how you use the story, not just how you tell it.

A good story does more than transmit information. It activates memory, anchors values, and connects people to each other. Done right, it does at least three things:

- **It stays with people**. Stories are remembered more easily than messages or charts—especially when they include context, senses, and emotion. The richer the story, the deeper the imprint.
- **It creates visibility**. When you tell a story that includes someone's actions, they become the protagonist. They're seen. They matter. And others take notice: *"I want to be in a story like that."*
- **It models values through real examples**. Stories are one of the most effective ways to communicate expected behavior, cultural norms, and what "good" looks like—without sounding like policy or moralizing.

You want to activate value? Start with a story people can relate to, build on, and pass forward.

Remember the crushed doughnut? If you read that story in Chapter 4 and remember it now, then there's your answer. Good stories stick. And more importantly, they move people.

Activating value creation is far easier when people carry a shared understanding—a narrative they've heard that shows them how success feels, not just how it looks. A good story doesn't just explain what's expected. It celebrates what's possible. And that's how you invite people to make it theirs.

Questions Leaders Should Ask Themselves:

- Do I take the time to explain why we're doing what we're doing—or do I assume people already know?
- Am I telling a story people can relate to, or just repeating abstract goals?

- Do I allow others to shape the way we get there—or do I feel the need to control the process?
- When someone asks, "Why," do I welcome the question—or treat it as resistance?
- Is the story I'm telling inclusive of others' contributions—or does it only reflect my perspective?

Why This Practice Matters Through the Lens of Human Understanding

- **People think in stories, not slides.** Stories activate parts of the brain that data doesn't. They help make sense of complexity and allow people to organize information in a way that's memorable and emotionally resonant. That's why the best strategies are not only planned—they're told.
- **When people understand the "why," their motivation becomes internal.** Purpose should be used as a compass. When people see the logic and meaning behind a decision or direction, they are more likely to self-align and make better choices in ambiguous situations. This is where the power of "Share the Why & How" in the Value Activation Framework comes alive.
- **People gain energy from connection.** It's not enough to understand the big picture—people need to see themselves in it. When the story includes their role, their effort, or their relevance, it fosters belonging. They stop working *on* something and start working *for* something.
- **Control without context breeds passivity.** When people are asked to execute without knowing why, they disengage. Even talented individuals stop thinking critically. Inclusion, here, means letting people understand the reasoning behind the decisions that shape their work.
- **Co-creating the "how" builds psychological ownership.** When people help define the path, they walk it differently. They take responsibility, anticipate issues, and invest in the outcome. This echoes the "Invite Thinking" condition of the Value

Activation Framework™—true inclusion isn't just about having a voice; it's about being heard when it counts.

- **Narrative gives culture its stickiness.** Values remain ethereal until someone lives them. Stories turn culture into something visible and repeatable. When leaders use storytelling to model behaviors, decisions, and trade-offs, they are actively shaping how the culture is internalized and reproduced by others.

When people are invited into the story—when they understand why something matters and get to shape how it happens—they stop working for approval and start working with purpose. That's when alignment turns into ownership and contribution becomes personal. You don't need perfect speeches or clever slogans. You need clarity, inclusion, and honesty. Share the story, and let people see themselves in it. That's how you make it theirs—and that's how value gets activated.

Practice 4: Honor the Contribution

When people contribute value—whether through effort, learning, or leadership—they need to know it matters. Not through perks or metrics, but through genuine recognition. Honor doesn't mean applause, it means creating visibility. And if you know the complexities of your people's lives, you'll realize how often they put aside personal priorities just to add value to the company. Since this effort often goes unacknowledged—because after all, "it's their job," right?—people eventually conclude that the extra effort isn't worth it. And when that happens, value creation suffers.

To honor someone is to say, *"I see you. You added something real."* It reinforces dignity. It reminds people that they are not interchangeable, and that their work carries meaning beyond the task. And it goes a long way—not just in the big, visible assignments, but in the little things: the teammate who always offers a helping hand, the person who volunteers to organize information when everyone else is rushing, even the one who quietly tries to keep meetings on time and on track. These behaviors may seem small, but they have a real impact on the team. They matter. And the person should know they do.

Too often, recognition is reduced to surface-level rewards or public praise disconnected from purpose. But true honoring is deeper. It's about noticing the behaviors and attitudes that reflect the culture you're trying to build—and naming them with intention. Many organizations make the mistake of institutionalizing recognition to the point that it becomes background noise. It blurs into routine. It loses its meaning.

Be spontaneous. Be specific. Be prompt. And above all— be genuine.

That said, let's be clear: **not everyone is contributing in a meaningful way**. This is not about handing out praise for simply showing up. If someone is fulfilling their responsibilities, there's likely something to acknowledge—consistency, reliability, professionalism. But in every organization, there are individuals who chronically underperform, disregard quality, or opt out of team accountability. This requires a different kind of leadership response. When a leader fails to address underperformance, it sends a message that undermines everyone else's effort. Failing to act isn't neutral— it erodes trust, damages morale, and dishonors those who are carrying the weight. **Correcting what's not working is also a way of honoring those who are.**

Inclusion here means validating contribution in all its forms. When you understand what a challenge truly means to a person— when you take into account their context, their personality, their current circumstances—you begin to see their success through their lens, not yours. Maybe the task would've been easier for you. Maybe someone else would've done it faster. But what matters when honoring someone is not just what they accomplished for the company—it's what it took for them to do it.

This isn't about making everyone feel good. It's about making sure people know they belong—because what they bring is needed, not just nice.

Questions Leaders Should Ask Themselves:

- Do I regularly notice and name the efforts that drive value—even beyond results?
- Am I reinforcing the behaviors that reflect the culture we want to build?
- Do I make recognition timely and specific—or rely on formal reviews and annual awards?
- Do people feel seen by me—or only evaluated?
- Have I made it safe and normal for peers to celebrate each other—not just wait for me?

Why This Practice Matters Through the Lens of Human Understanding

- **Recognition is how people know they exist in the system.** It affirms more than achievement—it affirms identity. When someone's effort is noticed, it tells them: *You matter. You make a difference here.* This is the foundation of Acknowledging Identity, one of the core conditions for activating value. People need to feel seen not just for what they do, but for who they are becoming.
- **Lack of acknowledgment erodes motivation silently.** People rarely voice the absence of recognition—but they feel it. Slowly, quietly, they give less. They become more transactional, more distant. When effort is invisible, the emotional bond between a person and their work begins to dissolve.
- **Recognition builds cultural clarity.** People learn what matters not by reading values on the wall, but by watching what gets named, rewarded, and remembered. When you honor specific behaviors, you're not just recognizing the individual—you're reinforcing the standards of the culture you want to grow.

- **Celebration creates emotional memory.** Recognition—when genuine and well-timed—becomes a moment people carry with them. They replay it in moments of doubt, fatigue, or risk. It becomes a reference point that shapes how much they're willing to give next time. This reinforces both Belonging and Narrative Inclusion—people feel not only appreciated but remembered.
- **Peer-based recognition multiplies impact.** When celebration flows horizontally—not just top-down—it becomes embedded in the way people relate. It strengthens **Relational Inclusion** across the team. When teammates honor each other, the system becomes more than leader-dependent—it becomes self-sustaining.
- **What gets honored gets repeated.** Recognition doesn't just reflect value—it drives it. When someone is celebrated for going the extra mile, helping a colleague, or living a cultural value, others take note. It's one of the most organic, low-cost, high-trust ways to shape behavior at scale.

When someone is truly honored, they don't just feel appreciated—they feel anchored. They understand that their presence, their effort, and their voice matter. And when that happens across a team, value creation stops being a leadership push and becomes a shared rhythm. Recognition is not a final step—it's a catalyst. It tells people, *"What you bring is part of what we're building."* And when that message is clear, people give more—not because they have to, but because they want to. That's the power of honoring the contribution. That's how value becomes continuous.

Value isn't extracted—it's ignited. And only leaders who make space for others can light that fire.

Looking Ahead: Activating Value Is Everyone's Responsibility

Throughout this chapter, we explored the third pillar of effective leadership: **Activating Value Creation**. We began by clarifying what value creation really means—not just from a business lens, but from a human one. Value is not created by direction or control alone. It is created when people bring their insight, energy, and creativity to the table—not because they were told to, but because they wanted to. And that only happens in environments where people feel they matter.

We introduced the **Value Activation Framework** as a model to help leaders—and organizations—understand the human conditions that unlock contribution: when people are understood, heard, involved, inspired, and celebrated. These are the very conditions that allow value to emerge.

Through the four practices in this chapter, we translated those conditions into action:

- **Understand and Embrace What Moves Others**: Because people create value when their work aligns with what matters to them.

- **Make Room for Other Ways of Thinking**: Because innovation only happens when people feel safe to challenge.

- **Connect People to the Why and How**: Because context, meaning, and shared stories amplify commitment and direction.

- **Honor Progress, Not Just Outcomes**: Because recognition reinforces behavior and makes people feel seen—fueling sustainable engagement.

Each of these practices invites leaders to go beyond delegation and into activation—helping people become not just participants, but creators of the organization's future. But just as important, this is not only about what **leaders** do. These practices remind us that **everyone** plays a part in activating value. Everyone can be a storyteller. Everyone can create space. Everyone can celebrate what's working. That's what builds cultures that last.

Now that we've explored how to **Provide Clear Direction, Enable Capabilities, and Activate Value Creation**, it's time to connect these practices to the bigger picture. Before we shift focus from the individual leader to the broader system they operate within, we need to step back and answer a final question: *What do these practices actually build?*

In the next chapter, we will revisit the four outcomes introduced early in the book—culture, fluidity, value creation, and execution—and explore how leadership practices become the levers that bring them to life. Because leadership, when done well, doesn't just move people. It reshapes what an organization can become.

Chapter 8: Building What Truly Matters

Back in Chapter 1, we laid out what leadership is ultimately accountable for, even if most organizations don't name it clearly. Beyond dashboards and operating plans, there are four real deliverables that define the long-term success of any leader: a thriving culture, an organization that moves with fluidity, a system that continuously creates value, and, as a result of those, extraordinary execution of strategy.

Most leaders don't set out to undermine these outcomes. They are simply swept into the urgency of delivering results. I have seen this play out time and time again—long, so-called top leadership meetings intended to address strategic issues devolve into operational back-and-forths with no end in sight. Leaders become immersed in the how and when, losing sight of the people and priorities that matter most. Stakeholders vanish from the conversation. No one pauses to ask: How does this impact our clients? How are we preparing for the future? Who are we grooming for their next role? What are we doing about the low engagement and dysfunctional culture that we all recognize, yet quietly tolerate?

It's true that most systems reward performance, not legacy. But that doesn't change the reality. Whether recognized or not, these four outcomes are the hidden scoreboard of leadership. They are what people inherit when a leader moves on. And they are often the first things to erode when leadership is reduced to task management.

That's where the connection to practice becomes essential. Because none of these outcomes emerge on their own. Culture doesn't thrive because it was named in a values statement. Fluidity doesn't materialize just because smart people were hired. Value isn't created through ambition alone. These things are built—or broken—by the way leaders actually lead. And for that to happen, leaders must first become aware of the responsibility they carry to make it happen.

The leadership practices we've explored—providing clear direction, enabling others to act, and activating value through recognition and inclusion—are not just helpful traits. They are the operational mechanisms that make those deeper outcomes possible.

We've talked about the idea of building a lasting legacy. Now is the moment to reflect on what that legacy truly looks like. It's not about whether, in a given year, the company hit its numbers. That is a discretionary outcome, vulnerable to luck, timing, or external factors. Legacy shows up when systems and structures have been built in such a way that success becomes repeatable, even predictable. When culture reinforces behavior without being micromanaged. When people create value not because they were told to, but because the environment invites it. When employees wake up each morning believing, "My work matters. I have impact. And I am building something bigger than myself."

Practices vs. Functions: The Real Work of Leadership

Every leadership role comes with a set of responsibilities that are visible, repeatable, and directly tied to the job. Planning, budgeting, hiring, organizing, setting targets—these are the functions of leadership. They matter. They create structure, move decisions forward, and keep operations running. And, to be candid, they're usually the only parts of the role that get formally transferred from one leader to the next.

Think back to the first time you stepped into a new leadership role. If someone handed over the reins, what did they focus on? Chances are, you were walked through the systems, shown the key reports, briefed on the processes, and maybe given a sense of the cadence and mechanics of the role. If you were lucky, it was done with care and clarity.

But were you also brought up to speed on the human dynamics? Did they share insight into the team's strengths and tensions, the quiet politics, the potential waiting to be activated? Were you briefed on the deeper work—unresolved issues, long-term priorities, ideas in motion that needed nurturing? Did anyone hand you a talent map to help you see who was ready for more, who needed support, who had gone unnoticed?

If you did, I'm glad. Truly. Because in almost three decades of working with organizations, I've seen how rare that kind of leadership transition really is. Most people experience something far more transactional. The plug-and-play model: fill the vacancy, figure it out.

And in that silence—what isn't said, what isn't handed over— we see the problem. The assumption is that if someone can perform the function, they'll be fine. As long as they can handle the workflow, manage the meetings, and hit the numbers, they're doing their job. But that assumption feeds the very problem we're trying to change. We continue to prioritize short-term execution while neglecting what actually builds sustainability.

Naturally, leaders double down on what they know will show results. They ensure execution. They focus on what's visible: goals, targets, reports. They become highly efficient functional leaders, and in many cases, they're praised for it. But being a high-functioning leader isn't the same as being an effective one.

You can plan well and still create confusion. You can hire the best talent and fail to grow it. You can set ambitious goals and still leave people disconnected from meaning.

This is the blind spot. Leadership functions can be trained. They can be transferred, checklist-style. But practices must be understood, embodied, and lived.

Functions ensure that work gets done. Practices determine whether that work means something, whether it scales across teams, and whether it creates anything that lasts.

One shows what your job is. The other reveals the impact of your leadership.

How Practices Enable the True Outcomes

Before diving deeper into the true impact of the Core Leadership Practices, we need to acknowledge something we touched on early in the book: most companies aren't asking this from their leaders. And that, in itself, is 80% of the problem. If an organization never defines what the real outcomes of leadership should be, it leaves very little room for transformation.

Unless we start holding leaders accountable for more than executing a strategy—usually one centered narrowly on financial results—we'll never shift the reality most companies are stuck in. There is something far more powerful, more durable, and more consequential that lies within the scope of a leader's role. And unless we ask leaders to own that, we will continue to build fragile organizations dressed up in short-term wins.

Results are the rooftop. Culture, fluidity, and value creation are the foundation. And your daily practices are the concrete being poured.

168

Practicing leadership at any level is not only about fulfilling a role. It's about taking responsibility for the structure that must exist in order for a business to last a hundred years or more. That structure is not just organizational—it's cultural, human, and behavioral.

The **Core Practices of Leadership Effectiveness™** are what bring that structure to life. They are the behaviors that make it possible for a leader to influence not just performance, but all four of the True Outcomes: Culture, Fluidity, Value Creation, and Results (Figure I).

When I talk to clients, the conversation rarely starts with missing financial targets. That's not where the pain is. What I hear most is: "We're not collaborating," "Our culture needs rewiring," "People aren't growing," "We're not ready for what's coming." These are not minor concerns. These are strategic red flags. And they are all solvable—when leaders learn to practice their role with intention.

Providing Clear Direction

When a leader provides Clear Direction, they do far more than transmit information. They give the organization a way to think together. A well-communicated direction creates shared understanding. It reduces noise, aligns energy, and gives teams permission to act. Direction becomes a stabilizing force in uncertainty. It shapes decisions and behaviors without requiring control.

It also touches every one of the True Outcomes:

- **Extraordinary Results** become possible when everyone understands what game they're playing and how to win it. A compelling vision—especially one linked to personal meaning—mobilizes more than effort. It mobilizes will.
- **Thriving Culture** emerges when people know what is expected, why it matters, and how their contributions fit. Clarity creates coherence. And where there is coherence, trust and purpose can grow.

- **Fluidity** depends on more than collaboration—it depends on context. Without clarity, people struggle to coordinate, or worse, operate in silos. But when the goal is well understood and deeply internalized, interdependence takes root, and movement becomes natural.
- **Value Creation** flourishes when people know the destination and feel invited to shape how to get there. New ideas need space, but also orientation. Without direction, innovation becomes chaos. With it, creativity becomes progress.

Enabling Capabilities

Enablement goes far beyond support or delegation. It's the ongoing, deliberate effort to ensure people have what they need to perform, grow, and contribute meaningfully. And when this is present, it activates all four outcomes.

- **Extraordinary Results** are no longer the product of a few high performers. When a leader develops the full breadth of their team, execution becomes scalable. Relying on the capable few is not leadership—it's risk management disguised as control.
- **Thriving Culture** is made possible when people feel they are growing. Few things energize a workplace like learning. I've heard employees say, "I'm learning so much—I actually look forward to coming in." And when leaders empower their teams to create that kind of environment together, culture shifts from compliance to enthusiasm.
- **Fluidity** requires autonomy, and autonomy depends on capability. When people are equipped—through feedback, development, structure, or tools—they act without waiting, solve without escalating, and adapt ahead of the curve. The organization begins to move as a system, not as a hierarchy.
- **Value Creation** often lives in the untapped potential of people who hesitate to speak up, contribute, or risk a new idea. Enablement turns possibility into contribution. It unlocks what was

already there. And when leaders commit to surfacing and nurturing that potential, they open the door to the kind of innovation only empowered teams can generate.

Activating Value Creation

Activation is the emotional ignition of leadership. It's what transforms compliance into commitment. When people are seen, challenged, appreciated, and included, energy is released. Not just effort, but ownership. People bring more of themselves—not because they're required to, but because they feel they matter.

Its impact runs deep across all outcomes:

- **Extraordinary Results** are not sustainable through pressure alone. They require drive. Leaders who activate people through recognition, inclusion, and purpose give their teams the fuel to keep pushing—even when the task is hard or the path unclear.

- **Thriving Culture** is built when contribution is noticed, celebrated, and made meaningful. People stay in cultures where they feel they count. Activation ensures that recognition isn't performative—it's a reinforcement of values and impact.

- **Fluidity** is accelerated when activation reaches across formal structures. Energized people collaborate more freely, break silos, and offer support without being asked. They move faster not because of urgency, but because of shared commitment.

- **Value Creation** becomes exponential when inclusion is real. When people are invited into the conversation—not just allowed to be there—ideas multiply. Diversity of thought turns into better thinking, stronger solutions, and a wider lens for opportunity.

> *If you want extraordinary execution, build everything else first.*

None of these practices happen by accident. And none of them come to life when leadership is reduced to its technical components. A leader can set a strategy and still fail to make it resonate. They can assign goals and still leave people unclear about what success truly looks like. They can organize work and still struggle to generate any real momentum.

What we've been saying all along is that leadership is not only a position of authority or a list of tasks—it's a role of design. Leaders shape systems. They influence what people believe is possible. And the practices we've explored are not just helpful behaviors, they are the blueprint for building something that endures.

A Note From the Field

Let me step out of the model for a moment and speak plainly—based on what I've seen, year after year, inside real companies trying to get this right.

Please, understand this: your company needs you to take this seriously. Leading is far more than ensuring the processes are executed and the targets are met. Those things matter, but they're not the full story. They never were.

What's truly remarkable is what happens when a business commits to seeing leadership differently. When a company begins to understand that financial results are exactly that—a result, not a purpose. A reflection of everything else working well. When that shift happens, and it's sincere, I've seen organizations become more agile, more innovative, more human, and yes—more successful.

It sounds like a dream, but it's not. It's entirely possible. I've lived it. I've seen the impact of leaders who put their heart and soul into building something real. And I've seen companies change course—sometimes slowly, sometimes with surprising speed—when they stop managing symptoms and start investing in the system that creates them.

But here's the truth: leaders need the very same things we ask them to give others.

They need **Clear Direction**—to know what's expected of them, what they are truly accountable for, and what success looks like beyond the numbers. Most of the time, they're guessing. They're reading cues from systems that reward short-term wins, and they respond accordingly. It's not ill intent. It's human nature. People follow the signals they're given.

They need **Enablement**—not more tools or checklists, but development. Coaching. Mentorship. Feedback. Time to think. Space to grow. We ask leaders to manage complexity, navigate ambiguity, and carry the emotional weight of their teams. But we rarely acknowledge how little support they actually receive. Leadership is trial by fire. And far too many are left to figure it out alone.

They need **Activation**—the emotional fuel to keep showing up with courage. To challenge broken processes. To speak truth to power. To prioritize people even when the system doesn't make it easy. Leaders need to know that when they go beyond the numbers, they will be seen, supported, and celebrated—not quietly punished for doing the right thing.

In many companies, being appointed a leader makes you complicit in the system's shortcomings. You're expected to carry the dysfunction, not question it. That has to change. Leaders aren't a privileged caste that should endure silently. They are people—strategically placed people—who have the power to shape what comes next. But only if we let them.

So be clear. Enable them. Find ways to activate them. Because when leaders are aligned, equipped, and inspired, they do more than manage performance. They build the infrastructure for the future of your company.

Bringing the Model Together

Back in Chapter 2, we introduced a simple idea: that leadership effectiveness is not defined by a single skill or trait, but by the interaction between what a leader does, how they do it, and how they show up along the way. It's that interplay—between **Function**, **Practice**, and **Style**—that determines whether leadership is felt as a burden or a force for progress.

By now, that model should look very different.

The functions of leadership—planning, hiring, allocating, measuring—are essential. They move work forward. But they do not move people. They do not scale impact. They do not create legacy. That only happens through the daily practice of leadership: the way direction is communicated, capability is built, and energy is activated across the system. And even then, none of it sticks unless the leader's style reinforces the trust required for people to believe in that system.

These three elements are not accessories. They are interdependent. Practices give meaning to functions. Style determines whether those practices are trusted or rejected. And function is the ground on which both are tested. Ignore any of them, and the entire model collapses.

The outcomes we've been exploring—culture, fluidity, value creation, and execution—are the real-world reflection of whether your leadership model is working. They don't emerge because of intentions. They emerge because of behavior. Repeated, consistent, congruent behavior.

The Leadership Scoreboard

Here's the uncomfortable truth: most organizations don't actually hold leaders accountable for these outcomes. They reward short-term wins and punish failure quickly, often without ever looking beneath the surface. And so we keep confusing functional output with leadership impact.

But when you think of the leaders who truly left something behind—those whose teams continued to grow, whose organizations adapted, whose influence endured—you'll find that they practiced differently. Most probably not perfectly, but intentionally.

> *Stop rewarding the ability to deliver and ignoring the inability to lead.*

They gave direction people could act on. They built others instead of guarding control. They created room for challenge, emotion, growth, and meaning. They didn't do more work. They did the right work, in the right way, with the right people. And over time, their execution began to take care of itself—because the system had been built to sustain itself.

That's what effectiveness looks like. That's what legacy is made of. It's not charisma. It's not heroic effort. It's not the number of hours worked or the number of decisions made in a day.

It's practice.

Practices are what scale your presence. They shape what continues without you. And in the end, they are the only part of your leadership that outlasts the role.

Looking Ahead: From Practices to Personal Readiness

In this chapter, we connected the dots between leadership practices and the real outcomes leaders are meant to deliver. We explored how **Providing Clear Direction, Enabling Capabilities,** and **Activating Value Creation** are not just helpful behaviors—they are the operational levers that create thriving cultures, build fluid organizations, unlock value, and enable extraordinary execution. These outcomes don't happen by chance. They are designed through daily leadership, practiced with clarity, consistency, and intent.

We also reframed leadership as a role of design, not just responsibility. The model you now hold in your hands is far from theoretical. It is built from lived experience, and it reflects what organizations truly need from their leaders—whether they've been able to name it or not.

But now comes the hard part.

Understanding what leadership should accomplish is not the same as being ready to deliver it. And that's where we go next.

In Part III, we shift from looking outward to looking inward. We examine what it takes for a leader to truly embody the practices we've explored—to face themselves honestly, to confront their shadow, and to let go of what no longer serves. Because building something that lasts doesn't start with others. **It starts with you.**

PART III: LEADING YOURSELF FORWARD

Moving from Presence to Permanence

"THE TRUE MEASURE OF LEADERSHIP IS WHAT REMAINS WHEN YOU ARE NO LONGER IN THE ROOM."
— Javier Castillo Gil

Chapter 9: Facing Yourself as a Leader

We've covered the work: Providing a Clear Direction, Enabling Capabilities in your people, Activating Value Creation. But before we move toward what endures, we need to stop and ask a harder question—one most leaders avoid: **What part of your leadership might be getting in the way?**

I am not being rhetorical; it is a practical challenge. Leadership doesn't usually fall apart because someone lacks intelligence or commitment. It fails when leaders don't see themselves clearly. They move fast, form strong opinions, and collect early success—then plateau. Or worse, they lose the very people who made their success possible.

There's been a long-standing push to help leaders focus on their strengths rather than fix their weaknesses. And developmentally, that makes sense. Bringing a weakness up to an acceptable level often takes more effort than leveraging what already works. (*Buckingham and Clifton's* work in *Now, Discover Your Strengths* helped popularize this idea.)

But here's the problem: That logic only holds **if** you don't have **derailing weaknesses**—the kind that are hard to ignore, even harder to work around. And more subtly, it breaks down when your strengths themselves start becoming your derailers.

Any competency can turn into its own shadow when overused. Boldness becomes arrogance. Creativity turns into chaos. Political agility mutates into manipulation.

And that's where the real problem lies—because these behaviors are often the very things that earned you promotions and praise in the first place. So, it's hard to see them as part of the problem. Try telling someone to "be less creative" or "dial down your drive for results." It sounds absurd, especially if those are the very traits that got them where they are.

But what if we reframed the conversation?

Instead of challenging the strength itself, we look at what it **provokes** in others—and what it **limits** when left unchecked.

For example:

- *"Your bold thinking is a strength—now let's make sure the team can execute it incrementally."*
- *"Your results-orientation is valuable—but how do we make those results sustainable and repeatable for your team?"*

This isn't about questioning your identity, doing humility exercises, or filling out personality tests. It's about identifying the parts of your behavior that might consistently create resistance, tension, or disengagement—and that you've grown used to excusing. Because it's just the way you are. And because it's worked for you… until now.

We All Have Patterns. Some Protect Us. Some Cost Us.

No one leads in a vacuum. We bring our stories, our fears, our survival strategies. Over time, some of those behaviors get overused—what once helped us stand out now starts shutting others down.

Here's how it looks in practice:

- A leader who prides on high standards becomes impossible to please.
- A calm and composed decision-maker avoids confrontation, even when it's necessary.
- A hands-on mentor turns into a micromanager when stakes rise.
- A collaborative leader struggles to make hard calls when alignment doesn't come.

None of this makes you bad. It makes you human. But left unchallenged, these patterns start writing the script. Your team just follows the tension.

And that brings us back to something we addressed earlier in the book:

The decision to lead doesn't just come with perks and opportunities—it comes with real challenges. One of them is this: **You still need to evolve.**

Leaders don't get to graduate from growth. Every team is different. Every shift in context might require you to reinvent how you lead.

Remember the **Finished Product Syndrome**?

If everything around you is changing—economic conditions, workforce demographics, technology, internal structures—what makes you think your leadership should stay the same?

The practices remain. The delivery must evolve.

You will still need to provide clear direction—but the way you define and communicate it may need to change.

You will still need to enable capability in your people—but the approach, the support, and even the pacing may need to adjust.

You will still need to activate value—but no two people are motivated the same way, and no team stays static.

That's why understanding your own patterns—how they help you, and how they might be holding you back—is essential. Because the cost of staying fixed while everything else shifts is irrelevance.

Yes, it's work. And yes, it's uncomfortable. But there's little learning in comfort.

And if we're being honest—there's little future in avoiding evolution.

The Feedback You Haven't Wanted to Hear

I believe that, up to a certain degree, most leaders already know their gaps. They've heard them—directly or through whispers. But acknowledging them requires something uncomfortable: **letting go of self-preservation**.

The Mirror and the Lens

Throughout my career, I've had the opportunity to assess many managers and executives. It's always a rich experience—to dissect behavior, explore what drives a person, and understand how they see themselves. One question I often ask (framed in different ways) is this:

What feedback has stuck with you over time?

And what feedback are you still resisting?

Almost inevitably, I get answers that sound more like justifications than reflection:

"They say I focus a lot on details—yet I get a lot of praise for finding mistakes."

"I've been told I push people hard—but my teams always are ahead on results."

These aren't confessions. They're reframed as **strengths**, and they often are.

But the real question is: *Are they effective today? In this team? Under these conditions?*

Because sometimes, **the very strength you're most proud of is the one thing getting in your way.**

Self-awareness is difficult to develop—partly because we confuse it with self-image. We think being self-aware means knowing our intentions, our motivations, our emotions, and our strengths. But that's just one side of it. Real self-awareness also requires us to understand how we're experienced by others—and that's where most leaders fall short.

There's a key distinction: **Identity** is how you see yourself. **Reputation** is how others experience you. And while we tend to lead from our identity, others react to our reputation. That gap matters—

because people don't respond to your intentions. They respond to your impact. You may see yourself as decisive, but they may experience you as dismissive. You may think you're detail-oriented—they may experience you as controlling.

And the truth is this: People don't treat you based on how *you* think you are.

They treat you based on how *they* perceive you.

Sometimes, the very strength you're most proud of is the one thing getting in your way.

That's part of what makes getting a clear read on feedback so difficult. Most people simply aren't very good at giving it. They avoid discomfort, soften the message, or speak in vague terms that protect the relationship but leave the point unclear. Even those with the best intentions tend to dance around what really needs to be said. They hesitate—worried about hurting feelings, triggering defensiveness, or creating tension with someone they still have to work with tomorrow. So, the message gets buried. And leaders, especially those in more senior roles, rarely get feedback that's both honest *and* actionable.

But even when feedback is direct and well-intended, there's another problem: We filter it. We hear it through the lens of what we already believe about ourselves. And when it touches something we're proud of—a trait we've been praised for, rewarded for, maybe even promoted for—it becomes harder to accept. Instead of listening to it at face value, we reshape it to protect our identity.

"They don't understand the context."

"They don't see the whole picture."

"This is just how I lead."
"If I don't push this hard, nothing gets done."

Those statements may feel true. But they're usually **defenses**—ways to avoid confronting the uncomfortable possibility that what once worked for us might now be working against us. And once you acknowledge the real impact you're having, you can't unsee it. From there, you're faced with a choice: Change or ignore it and keep paying the price.

Self-reflection isn't a leadership virtue.

It's a leadership responsibility.

The Internal Tradeoff: What Do You Get in Return?

Here's a fair question—maybe even the one you're quietly holding: *"If I spend all this time enabling others, focusing on culture, developing my people... where does that leave me?"*

It's a valid question. One that most leadership books either ignore or oversimplify. And it deserves an honest answer—especially because, if we're being real, **the system doesn't always reward the kind of leadership this book is about**.

Let's acknowledge the reality.

- Many companies do promote results-oriented leaders—even when they leave bodies behind them.
- They reward those who push hard and meet targets, even if their teams burn out in the process.
- They often promote visibility over substance, urgency over reflection, and control over enablement.
- They praise performance, even when it comes at the cost of trust, culture, and long-term stability.

184

And that's exactly why effective leadership remains rare. Not because it's complicated—but because it runs against the grain of how most organizations are wired today.

This book was never about romanticizing leadership. It's about confronting the truth: The system may not reward you for doing it right—not immediately. But the alternative? It eats you alive.

Because here's another fact—one that rarely gets discussed: **Bad leadership isn't just bad for the team. It's brutal for the leader, too.**

When you don't set a clear direction, you end up repeating yourself, redirecting efforts, chasing alignment, and constantly explaining things that should already be clear. Your team becomes reactive. Your time evaporates in unproductive conversations. Your job becomes noise management.

When you don't enable capability, you become the bottleneck. You stay stuck in the weeds, solving problems others should solve, reviewing work that shouldn't need review, jumping into fires you never delegated properly. You may feel useful—but you're exhausted. Your team isn't growing, and you're not either.

And when you fail to activate value creation, your environment becomes heavy—and stagnation sinks in. Motivation drops. Trust thins out. People disengage. And suddenly, creating the new and different becomes your burden alone. The team stops contributing ideas, stops seeing possibilities.

It's like trying to push a stalled car uphill—on your own—while the rest of the team sits inside, waiting for the ride to resume. You spend more time managing energy than innovating, adding value, or moving forward. It's Monday and everyone's already thinking about Friday.

Maybe even you.

If you don't work on this, this is what your career becomes: Long hours. Chronic stress. Useless conflict. Low engagement. Pressure without purpose.

Who wants to live like that?

And let's be honest: When that happens, you don't go home energized. You go home worn down. Your personal life suffers. Your presence disappears. You miss the chance to be more than just a title at work and a ghost at home.

So, no—you don't lead well *because* the company makes it easy. You lead well *because* it's the only way to perform without burning out, to succeed without sacrificing your sanity, to grow your people without shrinking your life.

And here's the part that often gets missed: **Doing it right pays off sooner than you think.**

Leaders who create alignment don't spend their weeks untangling confusion—they make time to think, to anticipate, to play offense instead of defense.

Leaders who build capability don't micromanage. They delegate with confidence. And by growing others, they scale themselves. They open space—for family, for reflection, for development, even for rest.

Leaders who activate value don't chase engagement—they generate traction. They build teams that want to show up, contribute, and grow. Teams that don't just perform—they evolve. They create environments where work isn't just a contract—it's a place where people see possibility, take ownership, and move things forward.

Maybe you're the kind of leader who genuinely believes this approach won't work.

That people need pressure. That without a firm hand—maybe even raised voices and heavy control—nothing gets done. Maybe you've seen it play out that way. Maybe you've even been rewarded for it.

And maybe you work in a company that still celebrates that kind of leadership.

That promotes output over people. That tolerates fear-based compliance as long as the numbers look good.

I get it. That model still exists. And it can deliver short-term results.

But here's the question: **How long can it hold?**

How much of your success depends on your constant pressure? What happens when you're not there to push, to correct, to intervene?

Because like it or not, **you won't be in that role forever**. Everyone eventually leaves the room—by choice, by change, or by time.

And when you're no longer in charge… what remains?

If your results fall apart the moment you step away, that's not strength. That's dependency.

And there's nothing sustainable about that—not for the company, not for the team, and definitely not for you.

So yes, companies still have a long way to go. Many don't yet reward the right things.

But that's not an excuse. You still get to decide what kind of leader you want to be.

And if you commit to doing it right—clarity, enablement, and activation—you'll see the difference. In your results. In your team. And in your life.

Because the cost of doing it wrong is too high.

And the payoff of doing it right? It starts showing up fast.

You don't lead well because the system makes it easy. You lead well because it's the only way to grow without shrinking yourself.

Looking in the Mirror—And Doing Something with It

This chapter isn't meant to be heavy. But it is meant to be candid. Leadership isn't about being flawless—it's about being willing to evolve.

Here are three uncomfortable, practical questions to sit with:

1. Where do I consistently see tension, friction, or disengagement in my team?
2. What feedback have I rationalized, minimized, or dismissed?
3. What do people tolerate in me that I wouldn't tolerate in them?

When I work with team leaders on how they manage their interactions, I always warn them:

Whatever concerns you about the way your team operates may also be a reflection of how you lead them.

Granted, there are times when the issue really is someone on the team. As we've said before, those situations need to be addressed—not doing so also sends a powerful message. But don't use that as a default explanation.

Start with the mirror.

Consider where you may have inadvertently skipped a practice, assumed alignment, or failed to notice a change in the team's needs. Use the questions above to guide your reflection.

Take note of what might be missing. Then build a clear, focused plan to act on it.

You don't need a 50-point development plan. Start with one behavior to shift and commit to acting on it—visibly. Tell your team. Ask for their help. Own your progress.

Just opening yourself to the idea that you *can* influence your effectiveness through a single behavioral change is already a win.

Assessing whether you're delivering on the leadership practices isn't about judging your traits—it's about evaluating your ability to adapt to the needs of your team and the reality of your context.

It's okay to experiment. In fact, it's necessary.

Exploring new ways of leading is how you begin to liberate yourself from the boundaries you've unconsciously built.

If there's one practice you know you're not executing at your best—*act on it.*

Don't try to tackle everything at once. Pace yourself. But commit to real change.

You might be surprised by what you can accomplish when you lead with intent—knowing you're not just building a better team or company, but also a better future for yourself.

Because the leaders who grow are the ones whose teams grow with them. And if your team isn't growing… well, you can finish this sentence yourself.

Chapter 10: The Invisible Trail You Leave

You've seen the job. You've seen what it asks of you.

You've seen that leadership is not a reward, but a role. Not a title, but a responsibility.

And not about being the best, but about making others better.

We've walked through the work—how to provide direction, enable performance, activate contribution.

We've asked you to look at yourself—at what you reinforce, what you avoid, what you carry.

Now there's one last place to look: **What's left behind?**

Because leadership doesn't end when you stop speaking. Or when you leave the meeting. Or even when you leave the company. In fact, that's where leadership gets tested.

Not in your presence—but in your absence.

Have you ever thought about the people who held your role before you?

How many came before—and how many will come after?

Your company might employ a hundred, ten thousand, or more. But those are just today's names.

Over decades, a company becomes a living organism—people come, grow, leave. Some thrive. Some disengage. Some remember it as the place that shaped them. Others as the place that burned them out.

Leadership isn't just about guiding the team in front of you. It's about shaping the **environment they walk through**—and that others will inherit after you're gone.

Because long after your last decision, what you built—or neglected—continues.

Through the systems.

Through the standards.

Through the culture that becomes "how we do things around here."

This chapter isn't about adding another behavior to master. It's about what's already forming in your wake.

It's like walking on wet concrete.

Maybe you don't turn around to notice the marks you're leaving—until they've hardened.

And by the time they do, others are walking over them, following the path you unintentionally set.

This is the final lens.

Not about what you do.

But about what **remains** when you're no longer in the room.

Culture Is the Shadow of Your Leadership

Culture is often described as "how things are done around here." But on a practical level, culture is shaped—and experienced— through leaders. Through your tone. Your focus. Your decisions. Your silences.

That means what you reinforce, what you ignore, and what you consistently tolerate becomes culture—for your team, your function, your space in the system.

Remember the 7 Factors of Organizational Effectiveness. When they're aligned—when purpose, strategy, operating model, architecture, and people systems reinforce each other—culture becomes easier to shape with intention. But when they're misaligned, leadership often requires working against the grain. In both scenarios, **how you**

lead becomes a determining factor in whether the culture takes root or unravels.

You may be a first-line manager, a department director, or the CEO. The scale may differ, but the responsibility is the same. If you lead people, you shape culture.

And not through speeches or one-off workshops—but through repetition.

If you routinely avoid difficult conversations, your team learns to navigate around truth. They become careful instead of clear. If you consistently push for speed and output, people respond by rushing—cutting corners, skipping context, and redoing work that wasn't aligned to begin with.

But if you model clarity, if you remove blockers, if you invite contribution—you start building something very different. You create the kind of environment where people take ownership, speak up early, and extend trust to others.

Will You Be in Their Story?

When I work in leadership or talent development, I often go deep into a person's formative experiences. I ask them to trace the path—past companies, cultural environments, team dynamics. I want to understand what shaped them.

And inevitably—almost without exception—they pause at a particular memory.

A specific leader.

The one they admired.

The one they modeled themselves after.

They don't remember them as flawless. That's not what makes someone stand out.

What they recall is how that leader practiced leadership.

How they conveyed a clear direction.

How they created an environment of trust and growth.

How they activated the team—made them feel part of something that mattered.

And more often than not, they talk about the **culture under that leader**—how it felt like an umbrella, protecting the team from the parts of the company that weren't working. It was the leader's way of shielding, guiding, and holding space for people to thrive despite the noise around them.

I hear this pattern constantly.

And it always makes me wonder:

How many people who've reported to you might describe you that way?

This isn't a question to trigger self-congratulation—or self-doubt.

It's to point out something simple and profound:

What you do matters.

It touches people.

It shapes how they experience work, how they grow, and what they carry forward.

And the culture you create—however quietly—is a **force**. A ripple that travels further than you may ever see.

Culture isn't what's printed on a wall or recited at a town hall. It's what people learn to expect—especially in your absence. It's how they learn to behave when no one is watching. And often, it's a direct reflection of what you've modeled over time.

You don't leave legacy in what you say. You leave it in the footprints your habits pressed into the culture.

What Happens When You're Not There Is the Real Test

One of the points we've made throughout this book is the importance of defining what's expected of a leader. At first glance, the answer seems obvious: *getting things done.* But the trap lies in how we define *"things."*

Most leaders default to performance results. Numbers. Deliverables. Deadlines. And yes, that's part of it. But it's far from the whole picture.

Because those results don't just come from pushing harder. They come from what you build around you.

Real results include the **capabilities** of your team, the **culture** you shape, the capacity for **innovation**, and the **fluidity** of the system you're part of. And here's the critical shift: You can't deliver any of that alone.

You need a team that knows the path, can walk it, and believes in going further than expected.

You need systems that move without friction.

And you need a culture that outlasts your calendar.

And that's why leadership isn't always easy to evaluate when you're present. In fact, the signals can be misleading. People nod. They agree. They follow through—at least on the surface. But presence changes behavior. Authority shapes reactions. And often, what you see is simply a reflection of what people believe you want to see.

The harder truth shows up when you're not there.

Now imagine the opposite of that fragility.

Imagine you've worked diligently to set a clear direction—and made sure the team truly understands where you're going and how you expect them to behave along the way. Imagine you've invited their challenges, built alignment, clarified priorities, and helped them see their role in shaping the way forward.

Suddenly, your presence isn't a crutch. It's a multiplier.

Meetings move without you.

Decisions get made in alignment with what you've helped define.

People act, not because they're told—but because they're enabled.

And when you've delegated consciously—when you've coached others into capability—you begin to notice something even more valuable: You can unplug.

You can step back when needed.

You can shift focus without everything stalling.

You can host that executive visit from headquarters without losing momentum on everything else.

That's creating true system intelligence.

Because if you must be in every meeting for things to move, if decisions collapse the moment you're unavailable, you're not at the center of performance—you're the bottleneck.

And it might seem like influence but, in reality, it's control.

And control sometimes feels productive, even flattering. But it doesn't scale. It doesn't last.

Leadership isn't about being central to everything.

It's about building something that runs without you.

Lasting leadership isn't measured by how present you are. **It's measured by how well things hold in your absence.**

And so, the real question becomes:

If you stepped away tomorrow, what would stay—and what would fall apart?

You're Already Leaving a Legacy

Whether you realize it or not, your leadership is already leaving something behind.

Every decision you make—or delay. Every behavior you model—or excuse. Every time you clarify, avoid, protect, or engage—you're shaping something lasting.

You're not just managing the present.

You're laying down patterns that will persist long after your voice is no longer in the room.

Most people think of legacy as a moment of recognition. Something formal. A milestone.

But real leadership legacy is almost always invisible in the moment.

It shows up later, in subtle ways:

In how your team handles conflict after you've moved on.

In whether people feel permission to challenge the next leader—or fear them.

In how a new employee learns what "good" looks like, not because someone told them, but because it's how the team operates.

In how the company thrives because of the processes and culture you embedded in your work, your team, and your function.

These aren't memories. They're systems in motion.

And here's what makes it so difficult to recognize while it's happening: **You don't get to choose what your legacy is.**

You only get to choose what you reinforce.

That reinforcement—through standards, decisions, reactions—is what becomes culture.

And culture is what people carry forward, with or without you.

No one will remember every decision you made.

But they'll remember how it felt to work with you.

They'll remember if you made things simpler or more political.

If you created space for others to grow—or made it clear there was only room for one person to shine.

If you led a team—or ran a show.

That's what endures. Not your presence. Not your personality.

But what you made possible.

Legacy isn't about scale. It's not reserved for founders or CEOs.

It lives in every leader who takes seriously the weight of what they shape—even if no one thanks them for it.

The Practices Become Your System

If there's one thing this book has made clear, it's that leadership is not an identity.

It's a job—with a structure, with responsibilities, and with practices that shape everything around you.

And those practices aren't optional soft skills.

They're how culture gets built, how trust takes root, and how performance becomes sustainable.

When you **set a purpose and name the behaviors you expect**, you don't just bring clarity to the team—you create alignment. You make it possible for others to make decisions in your absence, because they know what matters. They've internalized the compass. And over time, those expectations stop needing to be repeated— they start to be modeled and reinforced by others.

When you **address what gets in the way**, you're not just solving problems. You're removing friction. You're building a system where people don't have to escalate every issue—because they've learned how to move forward, how to access support, how to adapt and improve. You've normalized continuous progress.

And when you **honor what aligns**, you're not just recognizing people. You're codifying what's valued. You're sending a message about what gets attention, what earns respect, what's worth repeating. Over time, this becomes a new standard. Not because you demanded it, but because others saw and understood why it mattered to you, and it began to matter to them.

These three practices (clarity, enablement, and activation) aren't leadership styles.

They're **cultural infrastructure**. They don't just guide individual behaviors—they start to shape how the organization functions. Slowly, almost imperceptibly, they begin to influence how meetings unfold, how decisions are made, how tension is handled, and how progress is measured.

They affect how people prepare for conversations—whether they come ready to defend or ready to contribute. They show up in how performance is evaluated—whether the focus stays on output alone or includes growth, collaboration, and long-term value.

They influence how feedback is given—whether it's avoided, weaponized, or used to strengthen capability.

And they change how success is interpreted—whether it's defined as reaching the target at any cost or reaching it in a way that builds something worth sustaining.

This is how leadership turns into culture—through the repetition of what gets modeled, allowed, and rewarded. And once that repetition becomes embedded, it becomes something more powerful: a ritual. A default. A pattern others follow, often without questioning it.

That's why your leadership doesn't just shape outcomes. It shapes what people believe is possible. It shapes the language they use to describe a good decision, a strong team, a worthwhile risk.

And maybe most importantly, it defines permission.

What people feel allowed to ask.

What they feel allowed to suggest, challenge, or create.

And what they quietly decide is better left unsaid.

These ideas are not theoretical frameworks to be explored in leadership seminars and forgotten on Monday morning. They manifest in real ways—day by day, decision by decision. Over time, they shape how people behave, what they prioritize, and what they believe is acceptable. They guide how teams interact, how risk is taken, and how failure is processed. I am not talking about philosophy here; I'm focusing on architecture.

That architecture doesn't come from a strategy deck or a culture statement. It comes from the habits of a leader. From what you do consistently—what you emphasize, what you let slide, what you repeat without realizing it. That's the scaffolding of culture. Not just what you build—but how you build it. And whether you intended to or not, that structure becomes the one others live in after you've moved on.

You're turning daily leadership into sustainable systems. And eventually, those systems **become the trail others follow**—whether or not they remember who laid it.

Leadership is less like a monument and more like a garden–what you tend lives on, even when you're no longer there to water it.

What Remains Is the Work

Leadership is often evaluated by the results you create while you're in the role—how much you moved the business forward, how quickly you delivered, how visibly you performed.

But that's only part of the story.

The more important question is:

What results will be created because of your leadership—after you're no longer there?

That's the real test of whether your work was sustainable. Not in the environmental sense, but in the structural one. Did you build something that others can grow within? Did you make decisions that created long-term clarity, not just short-term compliance? Did you shape a culture that will outlive your calendar invites?

Sustainability in leadership is about more than processes. It's about the systems you chose to reinforce, the standards you protected, and the behaviors you consistently modeled. It's about the way your team learned to think, act, and lead—not just when you were watching, but when they were on their own.

It's also about how well you prepared others to go beyond execution, and how you helped them evolve.

How you grew talent, not just filled roles.

How you fostered learning, not just compliance.

How you used your time in the role to create more capacity—not just more control.

When we talk about a leadership legacy, we're not talking about being remembered.

We're talking about whether what you built keeps delivering results—without you.

Not because you held everything together, but because you put the right things in motion.

You created a system that holds, adapts, and continues to add value.

You may eventually move on. That's inevitable.

But the organization, the team, and the work—those should still have momentum.

If they do, that's your real contribution.

And if they don't, it's not your absence that's the issue.

It's how you led while you were still in the room.

The Room

Thank you for walking
this path with me.

If you're still curious
about these concepts.
Meet me in The Room.

I'll continue to share more.
Just because you made it this far.

— Javier Castillo

Chapter 11: If You've Made It This Far

Some Reflections Are Worth Turning into Conviction

If you've made it this far, you've probably already challenged your own assumptions.

About what leadership is.

About how it should be practiced.

About what it really means to carry the weight of other people's performance, growth, and trust.

You've walked through difficult territory, conceptually and personally.

You've been asked to reconsider the belief that leadership is primarily about delivering financial results—regardless of what company tradition or conventional metrics may still suggest. It's about shaping the environment in which results can be repeated, elevated, and sustained by others.

You've seen the case for clarity—not just in what needs to get done, but *why* it matters and *how* people need to work together to do it. You've probably come to realize that ambiguity, left unchecked, costs more than time. It erodes focus. It weakens alignment. And as a leader, you're the one who must resolve it.

You've explored what it takes to build capability in others—without needing to be at the center of everything. You've looked at delegation, not as a release of control but as a path to growth. And you've recognized that this kind of development must coexist with the demands of performance, especially when pressure is high and timelines are tight.

You've reflected on how value is created—not just through deliverables or milestones, but through inclusion that breeds engagement, purpose that fosters commitment, and belief that unlocks innovation. You've begun to see that performance is not only what people do, but how they feel about doing it, and that your leadership plays a role in shaping that dynamic.

And you've looked at yourself.

At what you bring into the room.

At what you allow.

At what you reinforce—sometimes without even realizing it.

You've examined not just how you show up, but what might stay long after you've left.

So, at this point, maybe it's no longer about what you've learned. Maybe it's about what you believe.

What you've chosen to let go of, and what you're now willing to commit to. Maybe it's time to ask the hardest question of all:

Have you made up your mind about what kind of leader you want to be?

Because that decision—more than any framework, model, or methodology—is what will shape the path ahead. It's the difference between continuing to lead by default... and starting to lead by design.

From Execution to Legacy

Before you close this book, let's revisit a few of the questions that matter most, let's call it a Leadership Litmus Test.

1. Do you see leadership as part of who you are, defining your identity?

Or do you see it as a privilege and a responsibility you choose to carry, one with clear expectations, practices and outcomes?
It's understandable why many people see leadership as something tied to identity. After all, it's often framed as a reward for talent, a validation of potential, or a natural evolution of professional success. When you arrive at the role, it feels personal. It feels like a reflection of who you've become.

But here's the thing: The longer you treat leadership as something that validates you, the harder it becomes to actually fulfill the role. You end up performing instead of building. Protecting your image instead of enabling others. Making decisions that reinforce your credibility instead of serving the system.

When you see leadership as a role—something with practices, standards, and real outcomes—you stop managing perception and start managing conditions. You move your focus from being impressive to being useful. From defending your place to creating space for others.

That shift changes what you do, how you show up, and what you pay attention to.

It moves leadership from something you prove to something you practice.

And over time, that's what separates those who are respected for *who they are* from those who are remembered for *what they made possible.*

> The more you try to prove you're a leader, the more you drift from what matters: practicing it.

205

2. Can you lead others effectively without really understanding human behavior?

It's tempting to believe that leadership is mostly about clarity of goals, strength of vision, or the ability to make sound decisions under pressure. Those things matter. But even the best strategy will fall flat if it's not connected to the people who have to execute it.

The fact of the matter is you lead human beings. Not functions. Not roles. Not headcount.

That means understanding behavior isn't optional—it's fundamental.

It's not a soft skill. It's what allows you to distinguish between what someone says and what they mean, between surface compliance and genuine commitment. It's how you recognize when resistance is masking fear, when silence is signaling disconnection, and when performance issues are rooted in something deeper than capability.

Many leaders are uncomfortable with this. They'd rather stay in the realm of plans, metrics, and models—things that feel objective, manageable, and clear. But leadership isn't clean. It lives in emotion, perception, and interaction. And the more senior you get, the more your work is filtered through other people's experiences of you.

You don't need to be a psychologist. But you do need to pay attention.

To what motivates. To what shuts people down. To how trust is built—and broken.

Because when you understand behavior, you stop reacting to symptoms and start seeing systems.

You stop guessing what people need and start building environments that bring out their best.

And you stop trying to lead everyone the same way—and start leading people in ways that work for them.

You don't have to master everything about human behavior. But you do have to care enough to learn.

Because without that lens, your leadership will always be reactive. And you'll keep wondering why things fall apart—when in truth, they were never fully held together to begin with.

3. Is leadership about delivering results—or about building the system that makes results repeatable?

Performance has long been the default metric for leadership. If results are strong, the assumption is that the leader must be effective.

And if the numbers are impressive, few people stop to ask *how* they were achieved—or at what cost.

But here's the hard truth:

Performance on its own doesn't tell you whether leadership is working. It only tells you that something got delivered, it doesn't tell you whether the team is burning out. It doesn't show you the rework, the silos, the disengagement, or the trust erosion that may be quietly compounding under the surface.

Yes, results matter. They always will. But what creates results— *again and again*—is not just drive. It's structure.

When leaders neglect systems (when they overlook interdependencies, bypass culture, or stay fixated on the urgent) they might hit a few targets. But they often leave behind a trail of confusion, inconsistency, and friction. The team may deliver under pressure, but they don't develop the conditions to perform without it. They get through this quarter, but they can't scale what they've built. That's the difference between effort and architecture.

Squeezing harder might get you one more milestone.

But shaping systems—how work flows, how decisions are made, how accountability is distributed—that's what makes performance *repeatable.*

It's not about creating bureaucracy. It's about reducing friction. It's about helping people do the right work in the right way, without having to fight the system to do it.

207

And here's where the challenge becomes real for most leaders: They confuse hustle for health. They reward output but ignore the environment that produced it. And then they're surprised when the next challenge exposes the cracks.

But strong leadership doesn't just drive results. It builds the conditions that make strong results possible—without grinding the machine down.

Stop getting into operational detail, and start building leadership at scale.

Because it's the only kind that lasts.

4. Should your value be measured by what you achieve—or by what others achieve because of you?

It's easy to confuse leadership with personal performance. Especially in high-achieving environments where competence and visibility often go hand in hand, and rising through the ranks has rewarded being the one with the answers.

But when you step into a true leadership role, the game changes. Your success shouldn't be measured solely by how well you perform—but by how well others perform because of the systems, culture, and support you've created.

That shift is harder than it sounds.

Because it asks you to redefine where your value comes from. If you've spent years being the expert, the solver, the one who steps in when things get hard, it can feel unnatural, maybe even irresponsible, to step back and let others lead.

The reality is more challenging:

If you always have to be in the room for things to work, you're not leading—you're bottlenecking.

If you have to make every decision, solve every problem, answer every question, then you haven't built a team—you've built a dependency loop.

And it will exhaust you. Eventually, it will fail you.

Scaling leadership means letting go of the need to be central. It means spending less time showing what you know and more time teaching others how to think.

It means shifting from **directing to developing**, from **knowing to listening**, from **solving to building problem-solvers**.

It doesn't mean disappearing.

It means designing yourself out of the middle, so others can operate with confidence, clarity, and autonomy.

That's the paradox:

The more you invest in enabling others, the more expansive your impact becomes.

Not because you're everywhere, but because your leadership is.

You don't scale by cloning your behavior or micromanaging every task.

You scale by equipping people to make decisions in alignment with what matters most—without waiting for your permission to act.

That's how leadership compounds.

Not through presence. Through propagation.

5. Are you prepared to be forgotten—but still leave something that works?

This might be the most uncomfortable truth in leadership—not because it's hidden, but because it challenges something we're rarely asked to question: our desire to be remembered.

Most people don't enter leadership roles thinking about legacy. But once they're in the seat—navigating complexity, managing expectations, and giving their best—it's natural to want the effort to mean something. It's natural to want credit for the systems you fixed, the team you shaped, the decisions that moved things forward. After all, you showed up. You cared. You sacrificed.

But at some point, real leadership asks you to confront a different question—not whether your name will be remembered, but whether what you built will keep delivering long after your name is gone.

While not every detail will be remembered, leadership often leaves a deeper imprint than we realize.

People may not recall your sharpest presentation or how many hours you worked, but they will remember how they operated under your leadership. They'll remember the standards you enforced, the space you created, the clarity you provided when things felt uncertain. They'll remember if they grew because of you—or shrank around you.

And even more than memory, they'll carry the systems you helped shape.

They'll work inside the culture you reinforced or even replicate it when they move on.

They'll move within the permissions you created—or feel the weight of the ones you withheld.

Because what lasts is not just your story.

It's the structure you leave behind.

And in that way, leadership leaves a mark whether you intend to or not.

The only question is whether the mark you leave builds momentum—or stalls it.

If your influence depends on your presence, it disappears with your absence.

But if your leadership has shaped how others think, act, and lead, then it doesn't need to carry your name. It carries your design.

This is not about disappearing. It's about making something that doesn't. It's about building in a way that others can grow from, extend, and eventually pass on.

Not because they're trying to honor you—but because the system works.

So maybe the question isn't, *"Are you willing to be forgotten?"* Maybe it's, *"Are you willing to be useful in ways that outlast recognition?"*

Because that's what leadership ultimately demands: A contribution that doesn't draw attention to you but keeps serving others long after you've stepped out of the room.

Legacy isn't about being remembered. It's about building something that keeps working— even if no one knows you started it.

What These Reflections Add Up To

If you've paused with each of these questions, you've probably noticed something:

They're not just about leadership practices. They're about how you think, what you value, and what you're willing to let go of.

They're about moving from instinct to intention.

From proving yourself to building something that frees others.

From managing the present to shaping what continues long after you're gone.

Each question offers a different lens, but they all circle back to the same truth:

Leadership is not defined by your presence. It's defined by your impact.

And not just the immediate impact of a result, but the enduring impact of what you enable, reinforce, and set in motion.

These aren't just philosophical reflections.

They're practical thresholds.

Because once you cross into this view of leadership—once you stop asking, *"What do I need to deliver today?"* and start asking, *"What will this decision leave behind?"* your entire posture changes.

And that's when the real work begins.

The Final Passage

This book hasn't asked you to be perfect.

It hasn't even asked you to change everything.

It's asked you to decide.

To decide whether you'll treat leadership as a position to protect—or as a role to grow into.

To decide whether your time in the seat will be only about delivering today—or also about shaping what continues tomorrow.

To decide whether you'll lead for recognition—or lead in a way that makes others stronger, even if they forget your name.

Because while not every leader is remembered by name, the best ones are remembered by the way they made people better, by the clarity they created, the trust they built, and the momentum they left behind.

You don't need to be at the center of everything.

But you do need to decide what kind of center you want to be:

One that everything revolves around—or one that holds everything together, even when you step away.

Leadership isn't just about how you show up.

It's about what you leave behind.

So, lead today like someone else's tomorrow depends on it—because it does.

And remember:

The true measure of leadership is not only what happens when you're not in the room—It's what remains when you're no longer in it.

Author's Note

My path into leadership development didn't begin with management theory. It started with systems.

I studied Computer Systems Engineering, where logic, structure, and predictability were the foundation. Everything had an input, a process, and an outcome. But soon after graduating, I became involved in a project that challenged that simplicity. We were translating the work of expert consultants in an assessment center into a programmed matrix that could map behavioral tendencies—creating structured patterns from the complexities of human nature.

At the time (1995), this kind of work was still uncommon. While behavioral assessments had existed for a couple of decades, their widespread systematization and scalability (especially within mid- and large-sized organizations) were just beginning to gain traction. What's now seen as standard practice was, back then, an emerging frontier. That novelty is what drew me in. The idea that personality could be structured, interpreted, and even predicted through systems was incredibly appealing to my engineering mindset.

But the more I worked with behavioral science, the more I realized how misleading that assumption could be. People are not predictable machines. They come with histories, habits, context—and, inconveniently for system designers—free will.

Over time, my curiosity deepened. I studied more. I worked with different companies and saw how behavioral models, while helpful, often failed to account for the quirks and contradictions of real human interaction. Corporate politics, team dynamics, and cultural norms all complicated the math. And yet, they were the very things leaders had to navigate.

I often joke with participants in my sessions that people have an unfortunate tendency to behave like human beings: unpredictably. That's the challenge—and the beauty—of leading them.

Later, during a master's program in International HR Leadership at Rutgers University in New Jersey, I found myself surrounded by professionals from different industries, countries, and cultures. When I described the frustrations I faced: leaders not giving direction, avoiding giving feedback, reducing their role to short-term performance, I expected it to be a local or cultural issue. But everyone in the group, regardless of context, described the same challenges.

That was the moment the foundation for this book was laid.

Over the course of my career—leading and building consulting practices at organizations like Hewitt Associates®, WKC Group®, Korn Ferry®, Hay Group®, and now The Morphing Group®, I've had the privilege of working alongside leaders across regions, industries, and organizational stages. And the patterns, despite all the differences, have been strikingly similar.

What started as frustration evolved into a framework—one that redefined what effective leadership looks like and what organizations need to function effectively, not just efficiently. That framework eventually expanded into new models for team effectiveness, organizational fluidity, and cultural alignment.

But this book isn't just the result of frameworks. It's the result of seeing, over and over again, what happens when leadership is treated as an *identity* instead of as a *role*. When performance is rewarded, but systems are ignored. When leaders are treated as plug-and-play solutions or promoted without being prepared or coached to lead effectively.

This book is my attempt to reframe that conversation. To bring leadership back to what it really is: not a position to protect, but a system to shape.

Not a performance to deliver, but a privilege and a responsibility to fulfill.

And it's a system that requires full involvement—from the organization, the top leadership team, and the leaders themselves.

Thank you for making it to the end.

Thank you for doing the work.

— Javier Castillo Gil

About The Author

Javier Castillo Gil
Leadership Advisor • Organizational Strategist • Author

Javier Castillo is a leadership and organizational consultant with 25 years of experience helping senior executives and teams transform how they lead, align, and build organizations that thrive beyond them.

He is the co-founder of The Morphing Group, a consulting firm dedicated to helping leaders design fluid, sustainable organizations through clarity, cohesion, and behavioral change. His work blends strategic thinking with a deep understanding of human systems, combining frameworks with reflection to enable real transformation.

Javier has advised leaders across Latin America, the U.S., and Europe, supporting large-scale cultural shifts, leadership development journeys, and executive team alignment.

He believes leadership is not a title, but something you practice—and that the true measure of a leader is what endures when they're no longer in the room.

Connect with him on LinkedIn:
linkedin.com/in/javier-castillo-gil-mngmnt-consultant

Acknowledgements

No work like this is ever truly individual. While I've carried the frameworks, experience, stories, and convictions in these pages, I've been surrounded—often quietly—by people who've made this book possible.

To my wife, Claudia (Vare), who encouraged me to pursue the dream of founding Working Knowledge Consulting Group®, and whose trust allowed me to build a company based on the very frameworks that evolved into this book. As a psychologist, she's been my toughest audience—and my most generous supporter, cheerleader, and partner in crime. Her passion, patience, and ability to challenge me when it matters most have shaped this work more than she probably realizes.

To my children, Sam and Celeste, who unknowingly helped me test-drive the future of leadership. Their questions, energy, and evolving worldview have been a window into how the next generation thinks, decides, and leads. Sam, your artistic talent gave this book its face—thank you for crafting a cover that speaks beyond words. Celeste, your insights and encouragement—especially as I found my way through the writing process—pushed me to finish strong. Your support has meant more than I've ever said aloud.

To my partners at The Morphing Group—Sergi and Hugo—who embraced these ideas as their own and have helped strengthen and expand them. Your conviction in what real leadership can be has been a powerful force in bringing these principles to more organizations and making them part of our shared work.

To my classmates from the Master's in International HR Leadership at Rutgers University—thank you for being an extraordinary part of my leadership journey. Our conversations—sometimes formal, often spontaneous, and always rich—challenged assumptions, broadened perspectives, and deepened my understanding of the global HR landscape. All of you were leading people functions in world-class companies across different regions, and your insights elevated the way I think about leadership, culture, and organizational impact.

To the faculty: Thank you for your intellectual rigor, your willingness to challenge my thinking, and your insistence on clarity and depth. Your influence is woven into many of the ideas that shaped this book—even if uncredited on the surface, your questions live in the subtext of each chapter.

To every boss I've had—whether inspiring or ineffective—you all taught me something. Sometimes what to emulate. Sometimes what to avoid. I'm grateful for both.

To every person I've had the privilege of leading or collaborating with: The words in this book may be mine, but the lessons come from you. From the mistakes I made, the conversations we had, and the growth we experienced together.

To my clients—both organizations and individuals—thank you for engaging with these ideas, often before they had a name. You've challenged them, implemented them, and refined them through real-world complexity. Your feedback through execution has been a vital part of this book's evolution—and of mine.

And to every person who contributed to the creation and production of this work—thank you for your dedication, precision, and belief in the message. Special thanks to Sarah Cisco, whose editorial guidance sharpened the clarity, rhythm, and confidence of this book.

Writing about leadership is easier than practicing it. I know that firsthand. Many of the ideas in this book have challenged me just as

much as I hope they challenge you. I've struggled with the very practices I promote, and I'm still in the process of growing into the kind
of leader I want to be. Yes, I believe I still have time.

But if there's one thing I've learned, it's that leadership isn't
something you master.

It's something you keep showing up for.

Thank you to everyone who helped me keep showing up.

— Javier Castillo Gil

References

Barrero, José Maria, Nicholas Bloom, and Steven J. Davis. "Why Working from Home Will Stick." NBER Working Paper No. 28731. April 2021. https://www.nber.org/papers/w28731.

Bennis, Warren. On Becoming a Leader. New York: Basic Books, 1989.

Bloom, Nicholas, James Liang, John Roberts, and Zhichun Jenny Ying. "Does Working from Home Work? Evidence from a Chinese Experiment." Quarterly Journal of Economics 130, no. 1 (2015): 165–218.

Bucy, Michael, Bill Schaninger, and Brooke Weddle. "The Science Behind Successful Organizational Transformations." McKinsey & Company, April 2015. https://www.mckinsey.com/capabilities/people-and-organizational-performance/our-insights/successful-transformations.

Center for Creative Leadership. "The 70-20-10 Rule for Leadership Development." Leading Effectively. Accessed April 25, 2025. https://www.ccl.org/articles/leading-effectively-articles/70-20-10-rule/.

Charan, Ram, Stephen Drotter, and James Noel. The Leadership Pipeline: How to Build the Leadership Powered Company. San Francisco: Jossey-Bass, 2001.

Colvin, Geoff. Talent Is Overrated: What Really Separates World-Class Performers from Everybody Else. New York: Portfolio, 2008.

Development Dimensions International. Global Leadership Forecast 2023. DDI, 2023. https://www.ddiworld.com/global-leadership-forecast-2023.

Expert Market Research. United States Leadership Development Program Market Size & Share 2034. Accessed June 10, 2025. https://www.expertmarketresearch.com/reports/united-states-leadership-development-program-market.

Freeman, R. Edward. Strategic Management: A Stakeholder Approach. Boston: Pitman, 1984.

Future Market Insights. Leadership Development Program Market Size & Trends 2025–2035. June 5, 2025. https://www.futuremarketinsights.com/reports/leadership-development-program-market.

Gallup. State of the American Manager: Analytics and Advice for Leaders. Washington, D.C.: Gallup, Inc., 2015. https://www.gallup.com/services/182138/state-american-manager-report.aspx.

———. State of the Global Workplace 2024. Washington, D.C.: Gallup, 2024. https://www.gallup.com/workplace/393497/world-trillion-workplace-problem.aspx.

Goldsmith, Marshall. What Got You Here Won't Get You There: How Successful People Become Even More Successful. New York: Hyperion, 2007.

Goleman, Daniel. Emotional Intelligence: Why It Can Matter More Than IQ. New York: Bantam Books, 1995.

Hamel, Gary, and Michele Zanini. Humanocracy: Creating Organizations as Amazing as the People Inside Them. Boston: Harvard Business Review Press, 2020.

Kayes, D. Christopher, and Anna B. Kayes. "Experiential Learning and Education in Management." Oxford Research Encyclopedia of Business and Management. Oxford University Press. Published online August 31, 2021. https://oxfordre.com/business/display/10.1093/acrefore/9780190224851.001.0001/acrefore-9780190224851-e-294.

Kotter, John P. What Leaders Really Do. Boston: Harvard Business Review Press, 1990.

Kouzes, James M., and Barry Z. Posner. The Leadership Challenge. 4th ed. San Francisco: Jossey-Bass, 2007.

———. The Truth About Leadership: The No-Fads, Heart-of-the-Matter Facts You Need to Know. San Francisco: Jossey-Bass, 2010.

The Morphing Group. Key Findings on Sustainable Success: 2023 Study on Engagement, Leadership and Flow. Part 1 of 2. January 2024. https://morphing.guru/resources.

Pfeffer, Jeffrey. Leadership BS: Fixing Workplaces and Careers One Truth at a Time. New York: Harper Business, 2015.

Pink, Daniel H. Drive: The Surprising Truth About What Motivates Us. New York: Riverhead Books, 2009.

Porter, Michael E. Competitive Advantage: Creating and Sustaining Superior Performance. New York: Free Press, 1985.

Reddin, W. J. Managerial Effectiveness. New York: McGraw-Hill, 1970.

Sinek, Simon. Start with Why: How Great Leaders Inspire Everyone to Take Action. New York: Portfolio, 2009.

Vargo, Stephen L., and Robert F. Lusch. "Evolving to a New Dominant Logic for Marketing." Journal of Marketing 68, no. 1 (January 2004): 1–17. https://doi.org/10.1509/jmkg.68.1.1.24036.

Wiseman, Liz. Multipliers: How the Best Leaders Make Everyone Smarter. New York: HarperBusiness, 2010.

Zenger, Jack, and Joseph Folkman. "How Managers Drive Results and Employee Engagement at the Same Time." Harvard Business Review, June 2017. https://hbr.org/2017/06/how-managers-drive-results-and-employee-engagement-at-the-same-time.

www.ingramcontent.com/pod-product-compliance
Lightning Source LLC
Chambersburg PA
CBHW022048020426
42335CB00012B/598